GLOBETROTTER™

Travel Guide

ISTANBUL

SUE BRYANT

NEW HOLLAND

Winnie O'Connor
Travel Consultant
410-667-6090 Agency
410-561-1690 Home

NEW
HOLLAND

★★★ Highly recommended
★★ Recommended
★ See if you can

First edition published in 2000
by New Holland Publishers (UK) Ltd
London • Cape Town • Sydney • Auckland

10 9 8 7 6 5 4 3 2 1

24 Nutford Place
London W1H 6DQ
United Kingdom

80 McKenzie Street
Cape Town 8001
South Africa

14 Aquatic Drive
Frenchs Forest, NSW 2086
Australia

218 Lake Road
Northcote, Auckland
New Zealand

Manager Globetrotter Maps: John Loubser
Editors: Thea Grobbelaar, Sara Harper
Commissioning Editor: Tim Jollands
Picture Researcher: Carmen Watts
Design and DTP: Éloïse Moss
Cartographers: Nicole Engeler, Genené Hart
Proofreader: Mary Duncan

Reproduction by Hirt & Carter (Pty) Ltd, Cape Town
Printed and bound in Hong Kong by Sing Cheong
Printing Co. Ltd.

Photographic Credits:
Hutchison Picture Library/Tony Souter: page 29
PhotoBank/Adrian Baker: page 19
PhotoBank/Jeanetta Baker: pages 10, 14, 39, 111
PhotoBank/Peter Baker: pages 8, 17, 30, 54, 70,
76, 112
Neil Setchfield: title page, pages 4, 9, 26, 44, 57, 98
Jeroen Snijders: cover, pages 7, 11, 15, 16, 18, 20, 22,
23, 25, 27, 28 [top and bottom], 33, 34, 36, 37, 38, 40,
45, 46, 47, 48, 49, 50, 51, 52, 58, 59, 60, 61, 63, 64, 65,
66, 68, 69, 72 [bottom], 73, 74, 75, 77, 78, 79, 80, 84,
85, 86, 87, 88, 89, 90, 91, 92, 94, 95, 96, 97, 99, 100,
101, 105, 107
Travel Ink/Abbie Enock: pages 6, 12, 21, 71, 72
[top], 83, 106, 108
Travel Ink/Marc Dubin: pages 102, 109, 110
Travel Ink/Simon Reddy: pages 24, 62
Elinore Wrigley: pages 35, 43

Although every effort has been made to ensure
accuracy of facts, telephone and fax numbers in this
book, the publishers will not be held responsible for
changes that occur at the time of going to press.

Cover: *Aya Sofya, Istanbul.*
Title Page: *View of Istanbul at dusk.*

CONTENTS

1
Introducing Istanbul

The call to prayer echoes out from hundreds of minarets just before the sun's first rays sparkle on the deep waters of the **Bosphorus**. Gradually, the roar of traffic builds up as the city comes to life. Ferries packed with commuters chug back and forth from Asia to Europe, while the first fishermen take up their positions on the **Galata Bridge**. The traders in the **Grand Bazaar** unpack their wares, ready for another day of fierce haggling, a way of life in Istanbul.

Istanbul has played a vital role in European and Asian history for over 2500 years. Straddling the Bosphorus, the narrow channel linking the **Sea of Marmara** and the Mediterranean to the **Black Sea**, the city guards one of the ancient world's most important trade routes. As a result, it is packed with cultural and archaeological treasures, from the riches of the **Topkapı Palace** to the splendour of the **Blue Mosque** and the incredible (and flawed) structure of **Aya Sofya**, first a church, then a mosque, now a museum.

In Istanbul, Eastern culture blends with Western commerce in one vast, chaotic metropolis. Haggle for leather in the Grand Bazaar, or browse the designer stores of the Alkmerkez Mall. Buy freshly squeezed juice from a seller on the street, or dance under the stars in a high-tech club on the shores of the Bosphorus. Explore the old wooden mansions on the **Asian side** of the Bosphorus, or admire the luxury holiday homes on the **Princes' Islands**. This crowded, chaotic city can be exhausting and frustrating but nobody could ever describe life in Istanbul as dull.

TOP ATTRACTIONS

*** Topkapı Palace: see the fabulous collection of jewels, artefacts and ceramics and experience the haunting beauty of the harem.
** Blue Mosque: exquisite Iznik tiles in the city's most important mosque.
** Aya Sofya: the dramatic dimensions and frescoes of Istanbul's church turned mosque turned museum.
** The Bosphorus: admire Istanbul's dramatic skyline from the water.
* The Grand Bazaar: thousands of stalls under one roof, a bargain-hunter's paradise.

Opposite: *Its minarets make the Blue Mosque one of the city's most graceful.*

The greatest part of Turkey –
about 97 per cent – is situated
in **Asia** but a tiny fragment,
comprising most of Istanbul,
clings onto **Europe**. The country's overall size is 779,452km²
(300,868 square miles), just 3
per cent of which is in Europe.
    Two of the world's
greatest rivers, the **Tigris** and
the **Euphrates**, both rise in
Turkey. The Euphrates is some
2815km (1750 miles) long.
But the longest river, which
remains in Turkey throughout
its entire length of 978km
(607 miles), is the **Kizilirmak**,
which flows into the Black Sea.
    Turkey has seven **neigh-
bours**: Greece, Bulgaria,
Georgia, Armenia, Iran, Iraq
and Syria.

THE LAND

Istanbul is part of the **Marmara** region of Turkey, an area
of rolling steppes and gentle hills. The city itself is built
on a series of seven low hills and is divided into the
European side and the Asian side by the **Bosphorus**, a
narrow, deep water channel that links the Mediterranean
with the Black Sea. The European side, in turn, sprawls
over the northern and southern shores of the **Golden
Horn**, a freshwater inlet flowing into the Bosphorus.

Seas and Shores

Around the city, the coastline is highly developed but
away from the metropolitan area, the shores of the **Sea
of Marmara**, part of the Mediterranean, are characterized
by scented pine forests and low but craggy cliffs, with
small sandy beaches. About an hour by ferry from the
city are the **Princes' Islands**, an archipelago of nine pine-
cloaked islands with pretty beaches, the four inhabited
ones favoured by the middle classes as holiday homes.

In the opposite direction is the **Black Sea**, a vast body of water fed by the **Volga**, **Danube** and **Dnieper** rivers. Water flows from the Black Sea into the Mediterranean and the Bosphorus, which is very deep and less than a mile wide, and has extremely strong currents. Pollution of the Bosphorus has been

rather a serious issue in recent years and a number of measures, some more successful than others, have been taken to clear it up. All vessels present in Turkish waters are forbidden to empty waste into the sea, although the law is not strictly enforced, and sewage treatment plants are under construction.

Above: *Büyükada Island is cloaked with fragrant pine forests.*
Opposite: *The old city forms a stunning backdrop to the Golden Horn.*

Climate

Istanbul's climate has dramatic variations. November to February are the coldest months, when the wind whips up the Bosphorus and the air is cloying and damp. Rainfall, and sometimes **sleet**, is heavy during these months and the layers of **dust** deposited by the previous summer become rivers of **mud**. **Air pollution** used to be terrible in winter, thanks to the use of lignite **coal** as the main heating source. This is gradually being replaced with natural **gas** from Russia and locals say the difference is tangible.

In spring, the city is at its most charming, with wonderfully clear, light, balmy days and pleasant evenings. July and August are intolerably hot, particularly for the amount of sightseeing most visitors want to pack in, with **low humidity**. The saving grace of these months is the *meltem*, a cooling **sea breeze** that blows down the Bosphorus from the Black Sea. Autumn is another good time to visit, with sunny days and few climatic extremes.

CLIMATE

Istanbul has strongly defined seasons. **Summers** are hot and dry, with daily maximum temperatures of up to 35°C (95°F). Midday may be difficult for sightseeing during July and August, but the evenings are wonderfully balmy. **Spring** and **autumn** are warm and sunny with daily temperatures averaging around 20°C (68°F) and are by far the best times to visit. **Winter** is the least attractive; as well as being cold, as low as –4°C (25°F), it is damp, misty and windy and the streets turn to mud. December, January and February are the wettest months.

Above: *Today numerous wild flowers grow around Gallipoli, where battles were once fought.*
Opposite: *Fresh fish is sold from stalls all along the Bosphorus.*

Plant Life

Istanbul is not a particularly green city; with 13 million people vying for space, there is little room for parks and gardens in the centre, and much of the planning seems haphazard. But along the shores of the Bosphorus, the suburbs are rich with **orange** and **lemon** groves and tall **cypress** trees. On the European side, **Yıldız Park** is packed with locals at weekends, while those living across the Bosphorus get their fresh air on **Çamlıca Hill**. **Tulips**, which originated in Turkey, flower everywhere in spring. Grapes, peaches, apricots and sunflowers are grown wherever there is space for agricultural land, although **cotton**, cultivated further south, represents Turkey's biggest cash crop.

Wildlife

Wildlife, hardly surprisingly, is not abundant along the Bosphorus, with the exception of countless sea birds. Fish stocks are better than they were in the channel, and towards the Black Sea there are several excellent fish restaurants. Look out for turbot, mackerel and anchovies from spring until late June and blue fish (or lüfer), striped mullet and bonito in the summer months. Tuna is fished in the Black Sea.

HISTORY IN BRIEF

The area now occupied by Istanbul has been settled for some 6000 years. A modest Paleolithic village evolved to become the capital of three powerful empires: the **Roman**, the **Byzantine** and the **Ottoman**, through a colourful and bloody history of invasion, slaughter, pageantry and power struggles. Strategically, Istanbul's position is unrivalled, guarding the division between Europe and Asia and the **Bosphorus**, the narrow channel providing the only sea passage out of the Black Sea into the Mediterranean.

NOAH'S ARK

American archaeologists are currently working on an exciting new theory that the legend of Noah's ark had its origin in the **Black Sea** area. The Black Sea was once a freshwater lake, but when sea levels all over the world rose after the last ice age, a massive surge of water rushed along the **Bosphorus**, causing the rock walls at its northern end to collapse, and rapidly flooding the lake basin with salt water. Villagers living around the lake were forced to take to the water in boats with their animals to survive.

The Hittite Empire

According to archaeologists, the earliest settlement is around Yarımburgaz, close to what is today the airport. Central Anatolia, however, was occupied much earlier, ruled around 1600BC by a Central Asian race known as the Hittites, who lived in a network of city states. Their capital was known as Hattusas, or today, Boğazkale, situated to the northeast of Ankara, where remains of the **Hittite** Empire can still be seen.

Greek and Roman Eras

The first documented occupation of the area, however, is in 666BC, when the Megarian King **Byzas** arrived at the mouth of the Bosphorus. Legend states that Byzas had consulted the oracle at **Delphi**, Greece, as to where he should found a city and been given the cryptic reply 'Opposite the blind'. The king spotted a small settlement at what is now **Kadiköy**, on the Asian side of the Bosphorus, and presumably thought to himself the Megarian equivalent of 'They must be blind', as the settlers had missed the obvious spot, on the hill where the **Topkapı Palace** now stands. This hill has spectacular views of the Golden Horn, the Bosphorus and the Sea of Marmara and is where Byzas chose to build his town. It was named **Byzantium**.

HISTORICAL CALENDAR	
1000–660BC The first fishing villages established along the Bosphorus	**1890** First railway track from Europe is laid
660BC Byzas establishes a settlement opposite 'the blind', on what is now the European shore	**1914–18** World War I. Turkey joins German and Austro-Hungarian allies
334BC Alexander the Great conquers Anatolia	**1915** Gallipoli campaign
196BC Septimus Severus demolishes the city walls and builds his own	**1919** Mustafa Kemal (Atatürk) leads the war of independence
AD324 Byzantium becomes capital of the Roman Empire under Emperor Constantine	**1919** End of the Ottoman era
395 Theodosius dies and Constantinopolis becomes capital of the Eastern Roman Empire	**1923** Atatürk becomes the first president of the Republic of Turkey
537 The Aya Sofya's foundations are laid	**1938** Atatürk dies
1204 The Crusaders invade Constantinople	**1939–45** Turkey remains neutral in World War II
1453 The Byzantine Empire ends with the conquest of Constantinople by Mehmet the Conqueror	**1960** Military coup. The constitution is rewritten
	1965 Süleyman Demeril becomes prime minister
1472 Topkapı Palace is constructed	**1993** Tansu Çiller becomes Turkey's first female prime minister
1540 The Ottoman Empire at its height	**1995–99** A series of weak coalitions and rampant inflation
1730 Great Janissary uprising	**1999** PKK leader Abdullah Öcalan is imprisoned; the Kurds threaten violence
1845 Galata Bridge opens	**1999** Massive earthquake on 17 August kills thousands in the Marmara region

Opposite: *Sultanahmet's Egyptian Obelisk once stood before the Temple of Luxor.*
Below: *The panoramic views across the Bosphorus are magnificent.*

Byzas' rule was shortlived; in 512BC the Persians arrived and occupied the town under Otonis, who had brought a massive army of 700,000 with the aim of conquering eastern Europe. He was never successful and in 479BC the city was once again Greek.

For many years to come, Byzantium was part of the **Roman** Empire. This lasted until AD196, when the city joined a rebellion in a Roman civil war and was punished by Emperor **Septimius Severus**. Septimus razed the walls, slaughtered most of the inhabitants and later rebuilt the city, naming it **Augusta Antonina** after his son, Antonius Bassianus.

In AD324, the city was invaded by Roman Emperor **Constantine the Great**, an act that was to shape the city's destiny for the next 1000 years. Constantine crossed the Bosphorus to Chrysopolis, now **Üsküdar**, gained control of the city and declared it Nova Roma, or New Rome, the second capital of the Roman Empire. The city was converted to Christianity (Rome was still pagan) and became the most important capital in the world.

Constantinople and the Byzantine Empire

When the city was in-augurated in AD330, Istanbul was named **Constantinople** and, like Rome, was built on seven hills. The surrounding domain was known as the Byzantine Empire. Many of the embellishments brought by Constantine from the far reaches of the Roman Empire can still be seen today, such as the Egyptian Obelisk on the Hippodrome.

Subsequent rulers added sections of city walls, as well as vast aqueducts and new defences. Attacks from outside were frequent, and occasionally from the inside as well. Much of the city was burned down in 532 during a revolt and it was after this great fire that Emperor **Justinian** had to rebuild the spectacular church, **Aya Sofya**.

Constantinople flourished as a centre for the arts and culture as well as political power until the 8th century when, under Emperor Leo III, a puritanical movement known as **iconoclasm** evolved. All religious images, including elaborate mosaics and brilliantly coloured frescoes, were smashed and plastered over, while nuns and monks were persecuted. Fortunately, this radical movement came to an end in 787.

The first Turks arrived on the scene in the 11th century, coming as nomads from the steppes of central Asia. Under an army general called Seljuk Alpaslan, the Turks defeated a Byzantine army and began a steady invasion of Anatolia. They were kept back for another 370 years by a series of **crusades** designed to unite the Orthodox and Catholic Christians, but eventually, in 1204, the Crusaders turned on Constantinople, killing thousands of Orthodox Christians, plundering the city of its wealth and sending the Byzantine rulers fleeing to **Iznik**. In 1261, the Byzantines managed to recapture the city, but in its much weakened state, Constantinople was never the same again.

THE CRUEL CRUSADER

Enrico Dandolo was the **Doge of Venice** and one of the commanders of the fourth crusade, responsible for the occupation of Constantinople in 1204. This was a grim period of the city's history, when thousands of orthodox Christians were brutally murdered by the Catholic crusaders. Before Dandolo died in 1205, he had insisted on being buried in **Aya Sofya**. When the Byzantine emperor recaptured the city in 1261, however, legend has it that his bones were exhumed and tossed to the dogs.

Ottoman Rule

The Seljuk Turks had now become a force to be reckoned with, growing from a small principality in Anatolia to a powerful army, known as the **Ottomans**, ruling over the Balkans, the area all around Constantinople and much of the remainder of the Byzantine Empire.

The fall of Constantinople can be attributed directly to the brilliance of **Mehmet II**, the Conqueror. In 1451, Mehmet prepared two magnificent fortresses on the Bosphorus for his invasion. Anadolu Hisarı on the Asian side was strengthened, while a second fortress, Rumeli Hisarı, on the European side, was constructed in just a few months. Together, the two fortresses guarded the narrowest section of the Bosphorus.

Mehmet meanwhile brought in master craftsmen from Europe to build huge **cannons**, and in May 1453 started to build up his forces around the walls of Constantinople. The Byzantines had installed massive chain links across the Golden Horn, so Mehmet took them by surprise. He bombarded the city walls by night and stealthily transported his ships overland, from a cove behind **Galata** where the Dolmabahçe Palace now stands, on rollers up the hill and down into the Golden Horn behind the chains. The emperor Constantine XI died fighting on the walls.

ART IN MINIATURE

One of the most important figures of 16th-century Istanbul was **Matrakçi Nasuh**, historian, soldier, calligrapher and painter. His intricate, colourful miniature paintings describe in fine detail the battle campaign of Süleyman the Magnificent in 1533, creating a wonderful atlas of the whole region. Of particular interest is his **painting of Istanbul** in Topkapı Palace, which clearly shows castles, mosques, hans, caravanserais and natural features like mountains, rivers and passes. The perspective is that of a bird's-eye view rather than a cartographer's, and it is fun to pick out monuments which are still standing today. The original, and many others, can be found in Istanbul University Library.

Mehmet entered the city on 29 May and immediately went to pray at Aya Sofya, which was cleansed and declared a mosque. Many other churches were turned into mosques, although those areas which had not resisted the Ottoman forces were spared. Constantinople was renamed **Istanbul**, which stems from the Greek 'Istanopolis', or 'to the city'.

Mehmet began the process of transforming Istanbul into a fabulously wealthy capital. He repaired the city walls and built a new mosque, the **Fatih Camii**, as well as Topkapı Palace and the Grand Bazaar. New districts of the city were established and seaside mansions constructed. Under **Süleyman the Magnificent** (1522–66) the Ottoman Empire was at its peak, extending from Vienna to the Arab peninsula and as far south as the Sudan. Süleyman's greatest landmark is perhaps the exquisite Süleyman Mosque, the city's largest, built in 1550.

> **GUILD SYSTEMS**
>
> The **Ottoman market** was comprised of guilds, tightly knit communities of experts with their own initiation rights, apprenticeships, mutual benefits and religious habits. Each trade had its own street, where its particular goods were displayed to the exclusion of all others, such as Fez-Makers' Street, Quilt-Makers' Street and Jewellers' Street. The guild system crumbled with the influx of cheaper goods, particularly textiles, in the 19th century, but even today shops selling similar merchandise tend to congregate in the same streets.

Decline of the Ottoman Empire

After Süleyman's death, the empire began to decline, falling behind Europe in technological innovation and under threat from Tsarist Russia in the north. The crack **Janissary Corps**, a much-feared army of former Christians who had been forcibly converted to Islam, rose up against Sultan Mahmut II in 1826 and was slaughtered en masse in Sultanahmet. This, combined with a series of weak rulers, meant the empire lost more and more land, and gradually Greece, Bulgaria, the Balkans and Egypt won their independence. Istanbul nonetheless retained a kind of faded glory, with some of the magnificent 19th-century buildings, such as the **Dolmabahçe Palace** and the Yıldız Palace, still popular today.

Opposite: *The fortress of Anadolu Kavağı is one of the many noteworthy sights along the Bosphorus.*

The Ottoman Empire

Dominions in 1322 A.D.
Dominions in 1451 A.D.
Farthest extent of Ottoman power (c. 1600)
Turkish Republic

World War I

Turkey entered World War I on the side of the German
and Austro-Hungarian forces, a decision that was to
prove a fatal mistake. The single bright spot in the
whole of the war was the successful defence in 1915 of
the **Gallipoli Peninsula** by a hitherto unknown colonel,
Mustafa Kemal. By the end of the war the Ottoman
Empire was in ruins, its armies totally defeated, and
Istanbul occupied by an Allied army. The sultan was in
the power of the Allies, forced to sign a humiliating
peace agreement that reduced the empire to a rump
comprising Istanbul and part of Anatolia, while the
Italians invaded Antalya and the Greek army marched
towards Ankara.

Opposite: *An old-
fashioned postage stamp;
the Latin alphabet was
introduced by Atatürk.*
Right: *This statue is a
poignant reminder of the
horrors of Gallipoli.*

Atatürk

Had it not been for Mustafa Kemal, there might not be a Turkey today. Most Turks rejected the terms of the peace agreement and rallied behind him in a war of independence from 1919–22, banishing the Greeks and deposing the sultan.

Mustafa Kemal founded the Turkish Republic in 1923 and took the name **Atatürk**, which means 'Father of the Turks'. The sultanate was abolished and the capital moved inland to Ankara, while Atatürk set about modernizing the country, abolishing the power of Islamic Holy Law, replacing the Arabic script with the Latin alphabet, banning polygamy and even introducing votes and equality for women. Western-style dress replaced the fez, the veil and the turban. Turkey had finally arrived in the 20th century.

Throughout the 1920s and 1930s, Istanbul played second fiddle to Ankara. But the city's natural resources, location and appeal, combined with a string of financial incentives to business, meant that under Atatürk's successors a wave of investment engulfed the city and Marmara area, bringing thousands of migrant workers. Atatürk died in 1938 but Turkey remained neutral in World War II, avoiding any further damage.

Turkey since World War II

The 20th century, however, was hardly the period of calm Atatürk had envisioned. The Democratic Party won the first Democratic elections in 1950 under **Adnan Menderes**, but throughout the decade the country fell into economic decline, to the extent that in 1960 the army intervened and a new constitution was drawn up. By 1965, the True Path Party was in power under the ultraliberal, nationalistic Süleyman Demirel, but the army had to step in once again in 1970 for a further three years. Bülent Ecevit came to power in 1974 and led Turkey into the Mediterranean island of **Cyprus**, occupying the northern third of the island and causing a seemingly irreparable rift with Greece.

SMOKING

Nonsmokers will have a hard time of it in Turkey, where enjoyment of the local **aromatic tobacco** is a national passion. However, antismoking restrictions are gaining ground, and it is not permitted on buses, airplanes, museums and mosques. The **nargile** or hookah is a tobacco pipe, one of the relics from the Ottoman era that Atatürk would probably have preferred to consign to the dustbin of history along with the fez. Hookah-smoking went out of fashion in Istanbul but has been revived due to tourist demand and can be practised in many historic cafés, including the **Pierre Loti Café**.

Yet another military coup took place in 1980, suspending all the political parties and also arresting their leaders. Turgut Özal, the leader of the centre-right Motherland Party, was elected prime minister of Turkey in 1983, and subsequently replaced in 1989 by his colleague Yildirim Akbulut.

The 1990s were a series of political musical chairs. Süleyman Demirel of the centre-right True Path Party was elected prime minister in 1991, where he stayed until 1993, by which time inflation was running at a whopping 70 per cent. In 1993, **Demirel** became president and Tansu Çiller became Turkey's first female prime minister. More corruption scandals followed and in 1997–98 there were a total of five attempts at forming a coalition, all of them unsuccessful.

The year 1998 saw countrywide celebrations of the 75th anniversary of the Turkish Republic. However, just one year later a colossal earthquake struck north-western Turkey with devastating consequences, tragically killing thousands and destroying countless homes in the Marmara region. Numerous foreign countries contributed to a massive rescue operation.

IN THE MOVIES

Istanbul crops up in various films. The city was, of course, the final destination of the **Orient Express** in Agatha Christie's *Murder on the Orient Express*, although much of the action takes place as the train travels through Europe. The city features in the 1963 Bond film *From Russia with Love*, starring **Sean Connery**, and in *Topkapı*, the 1964 comedy starring **Peter Ustinov**.

İstanbul in particular, and Turkey in general, come off less favourably in *Midnight Express*, the 1970s classic about a convicted **American drug smuggler's** miserable life in a Turkish jail and subsequent dramatic escape.

GOVERNMENT AND ECONOMY
The Constitution

The Turks themselves are the first to admit that their political situation is less than desirable. Since 1923, Turkey has been a **republic**, governed by a **national assembly** of 450 members. But the military exercises considerable power and often intervenes in political issues.

The **president** is appointed by parliament and serves for a non-renewable term of seven years. He has the power to dissolve the assembly and the right to veto laws and amendments to the constitution, as well as to nominate members of the Supreme Court. The day to day running of the country, however, is taken care of by the prime minister, who heads Parliament, which is comprised of the **Senate** and the **Chamber of Deputies**.

Politics

Turkey's big problem is that there are too many political parties – some 18 major ones in 1999, as well as countless minority representations – and too little power for any one party. A series of weak coalitions characterized the late 1990s, during which there were six governments in four years. In June 1999 a coalition government was formed between the Democratic Left Party (DSP), the Nationalist Movement Party (MHP) and the Motherland Party (ANAP), between them holding 350 out of the 550 seats in parliament. During this time, the only constant has been the Islamic fundamentalist **Welfare Party**, which now holds around 21 per cent of the seats in parliament. But with its anti-European and strong religious views, the Welfare Party has been unable to form a coalition. The **army**, in any case, firmly secular in outlook, will fight hard against a fundamentalist government and steps are being taken to reform the electoral system into one with two tiers, which will allow the secular parties to join forces and keep the fundamentalists out.

LOCAL GOVERNMENT

Local government has considerable power in each of Turkey's 67 provinces. A **governor** oversees each one, reporting to central government, to which he or she can also apply for loans and subsidies. **Local councils** have the power to raise taxes, which may differ from region to region. Their elected councils and **mayors** are usually representatives of the main political parties. Istanbul has had a fundamentalist mayor for some years, who has taken considerable steps to clean up the city, with significant results.

Opposite: *The Atatürk monument is a feature of busy Taksim Square.*
Below: *Turks are very patriotic and the Turkish flag flies everywhere.*

Economic Development

Turkey suffered rampant **inflation** during the 1990s, with soaraway figures of 100 per cent or more only being reined in towards the end of the decade with a package of strict anti-inflation measures endorsed by the International Monetary Fund (IMF). However, the Turkish economy is relatively sound and continues to expand, albeit at a slowing rate.

Istanbul lies at the very heart of the country's richest area; the Marmara region generates approximately 60 per cent of Turkey's wealth. **Banking**, **commerce** and **tourism** are growing in importance, with a clear shift in the private sector towards the **service industries**. Tourism generates millions of dollars in income from the city and in 1998 a new Visitors and Convention Bureau was set up to promote Istanbul worldwide in the lucrative congress market.

Turkey's future economic alliances look uncertain. The country is desperate to join the European Union but the barriers to progress are severe: first, the country's poor human rights record over 14 years of Kurdish rebellion and second, its relationship with Greece over Cyprus, a situation on which neither side seems likely to budge.

Below: *Istanbul has plenty of ATMs, even in places such as the Grand Bazaar.*

For now, Istanbul is strengthening its position eastwards, forging closer economic links with the former Soviet republics. Many **Russian** companies have a marked presence in Istanbul and a lot of western oil and gas companies with interests in central Asia have based themselves here. If Turkey is ever to become an important economic power, it will be in the so-called **Turkic Block**, the area immediately surrounding the country. The **Black Sea Economic Cooperation**, formed in the 1980s, is a nonpolitical body aiming to develop market economies and economic prosperity in its member states, which consist of Albania, Armenia, Azerbaijan, Bulgaria, Georgia, Greece, Moldova, Romania, Russia, Turkey and Ukraine.

Above: *The Bosphorus Bridge is one of the main arterial routes into the city.*

Infrastructure

Massive migration into Istanbul and limited space in which to house everybody means that the city's infrastructure is under rather serious pressure. Various improvement projects are underway but are constantly delayed due to a lack of funding. **Atatürk Airport** is being expanded, with a new terminal being built to handle international flights. Underground lines are being built to serve commuters (the present offering, the **Tünel**, is used mainly by tourists). There is also talk of a third main bridge being constructed over the **Bosphorus**, but with massive opposition.

Plans for getting **oil** out of the Caspian Sea will have a tremendous impact on Istanbul. The option that is the most favourable to the city, and also the most expensive, is to construct an oil pipeline from Baku in Azerbaijan to Ceyhan on the Mediterranean coast in southern Turkey. The other two options involve building shorter pipelines to Black Sea ports and shipping the oil through the Bosphorus, which will mean a huge increase in traffic on the already busy stretch of water and a potentially devastating effect of pollution.

ROAD RAGE

The **car** rules in Istanbul. Streets are clogged all day, all year round and the cacophony of horns soon recedes from an unbearable din to background noise as you acclimatize. Turkey has one of the world's highest rates of **road traffic accidents** and a fair proportion of them involve **pedestrians**. The bad news is, the majority of accidents are blamed on these hapless pedestrians and unless you are knocked down while you are on a crossing, you may not have many rights in the eyes of the law.

Industry and Agriculture

Turkey was until recently one of a handful of countries in the world that is a net exporter of **food**, although the agricultural sector has finally been overtaken by **manufacturing**. It is still a crucial sector of the economy, however, composed of 55 per cent crops, 34 per cent livestock and the remainder of forestry and fishing. Grapes, figs, citrus, cereals, tobacco and, primarily, cotton, are the main crops. Important **secondary industries** include engineering, domestic appliances and consumer goods, while the principal tertiary industry is **tourism**, which brings in over US$4 billion a year.

The balance between agriculture, manufacturing and tourism is slowly changing. Contracting overseas markets means that the textile industry, the country's largest, which accounts for two-fifths of all exports and employs two million people, is threatening hundreds of thousands of redundancies. Some sectors are thriving; the electronics and household appliances industry reported a 23 per cent growth in exports for the first eight months of 1998, accounting for US$1.222 billion of sales.

Social Services

State education, secular and with a technical emphasis, is free to all Turks at all levels. Istanbul has several **universities**, and private international **schools** as well. Illiteracy throughout the country is at 10 per cent, a remarkable turnaround from 1923, when the Republic was formed – then just 10 per cent of the population was literate. Basic **health care** is also free to Turks, although most opt for private insurance cover. Visitors should never travel without adequate health insurance.

THE PEOPLE

Turkey's population is around 60 million, with some 13 million of these living in Istanbul, although an exact census is difficult to carry out. The majority – around 98 per cent – are Sunni **Muslims**, although Turkey is secular by constitution.

Turkey may be Muslim in faith and the country may border the Middle East, but the Turks certainly don't see themselves as Arabs. The original **Turkic** people came from Central Asia where, despite being nomads, they ruled several empires before migrating to the west, arriving in **Anatolia** in the 11th century and conquering Constantinople in 1453. At various stages, **Armenians**, **Greeks**, **Arabs** and **Mongols** have settled in Turkey and mingled with the Turkic race, and the people today are a mixture of Mediterranean, Asiatic and, to a lesser extent, Arab in appearance.

The **Kurds** are the largest minority, numbering around 10 million and based mainly in the east. The Kurds, who have their own language, culture and traditions, have for years struggled for autonomy, to date unsuccessfully. The terrorist attacks on civilians and tourists throughout the 1990s by the **Kurdistan Workers Party** is just part of a bitter war, in which over 30,000 have died.

Istanbul also has a small **Jewish** community of around 20,000 and a **Greek** population of approximately 100,000, a figure vastly diminished since the Turkish War of Independence in 1919 and also the Cyprus crisis in 1974.

GOOD MANNERS

Here is how to make **polite conversation** in Turkish:
My name is… • *Adım…*
What is your name? • *Adınız ne?*
How are you? • *Nasılsınız?*
Very well, thank you • *İyiyim teşekkür ederim*
Do you speak English? • *İngilizce biliyor musunuz?*
Please • *Lütfen*
Thank you • *Mersi*
Hello • *Merhaba*

Opposite: *Tempting and colourful fruit markets can be found all over the city.*
Below: *Smoking a hookah in a café is a popular pastime among Turkish men.*

BODY LANGUAGE

When in Turkey, shaking your head from side to side means that you don't under-stand rather than 'no'. To say 'no', nod your head up and back, lifting your eyebrows at the same time, or just raise your eyebrows. Turks say 'yes' by nodding their heads forward and down. Beckoning is signalled by waving a hand downward and towards yourself rather than waggling with a finger. It is also considered impolite to point directly at anyone.

Language

Turkish is a unique language and consequently difficult for the visitor to learn. The alphabet used is Latin, albeit with several accents that visitors are advised to learn if they want to be understood by taxi drivers (*see* boxes, page 21, page 61 and page 124). Dialects of Turkic are also present, from **Azerbaijani** to **Kazakh**, although you are unlikely to need these in Istanbul.

Most Turks in the worlds of tourism or commerce speak some **English** and you may find yourself being hassled in **German** and **French** in the Grand Bazaar as well.

Culture

Turks are by nature extremely **hospitable**, although in Istanbul the time-honoured tradition of serving visitors **tea** in a shop before they take a look around has been somewhat **corrupted** in the touristy spots like the Grand Bazaar. Family life is very important, although Istanbul's culture has been more diluted by Western influence than that of other parts of the country. Women work and indeed, hold positions of power, although they may still eat in a separate area of a restaurant. Dress is fairly modest – it is common to see women wearing a **chador**, or headscarf.

Westerners should respect a few rules, even in cosmopolitan Istanbul. Don't **point** at someone with your finger; don't show the sole of your foot; don't blow your nose or pick your teeth openly in public; and keep public displays of affection to a minimum.

Below: *Muslim women keep their heads covered in public places.*

Religion

Daily life in Turkey can be confusing as it is typically Muslim in many respects and typically Western in others. For example, the Muslim **sabbath** is Friday, although business hours in Turkey, particularly in the big cities, are Monday to Friday inclusive. The only difference on a Friday is that **mosques** and **hamams** may be busier than usual. Shops and offices are closed on Sundays and museums are a law unto themselves when it comes to closing days, although many opt for Mondays.

Above: Prayer is a regular and essential part of the Muslim day.

Muslim, not Christian holidays tend to be observed but you will still see **Christmas** trees and New Year's Eve parties being advertised in December, particularly in the big hotels. And finally, although the **Gregorian** calendar is used in day to day life, the main Muslim festivals are all observed, following the **Hijrical**, or lunar calendar, which differs by 11 days each year.

Ramazan, or Ramadan, is the longest event, a period of 30 days in which no Muslim (apart from the sick, the very young and pregnant women) may smoke, eat or drink between sunrise and sunset. Visitors should show respect and avoid eating on the streets in daytime during Ramazan. Indeed, it may be difficult to find places that will serve food during daylight hours. Business carries on as normal, although you may find your contacts more than a little irritable by the end of the day from lack of sustenance – and cigarettes. Don't be put off visiting, though; there is an almost festive atmosphere in the evenings and many establishments prepare special traditional menus at this time.

THE BELIEFS OF MUSLIMS

The Muslim religion is straightforward. Its followers must adhere to the following simple rules:

- to say, understand and believe that there is no God but God, and **Mohammed** is his prophet;
- to **pray** five times daily at dawn, noon, mid-afternoon, sunset and after dark;
- to keep to the fast of **Ramazan**;
- to make a pilgrimage to **Mecca** if physically possible;
- to give **charity** to the poor in the form of a tax.

Above: *A performance of whirling dervishes is a spectacular sight.*

SECRETS OF THE KILIM

The **symbols** on the Turkish kilim rug are more than just doodlings; their roots are believed to date back to neolithic times and variations on each have been found as far apart as the Atlas mountains of Morocco and the Andes of South America. The **evil eye** is a folk symbol to protect the household from evil. A **ram's horn** symbolizes power and fertility, while a **wheat ear** or a **pomegranate** mean wealth. **Birds**, often used, mean freedom and news from afar. A **spider** motif goes back to the legend of Arachne, a maiden who was so proud of her weaving skills that the goddess Athena turned her into a spider.

Şeker Bayramı, or the **Sugar Festival**, follows immediately after Ramazan and represents three days of celebrations following the big fast. This is a time for families, and children are often given sweets and gifts. Tables are festooned with delicacies – according to tradition, over 40 varieties should be displayed. On the second day, everybody visits friends and on the third, people attend concerts and festivals, although this is more of a tradition in the villages than the big cities.

Kurban Bayramı, or the **Feast of the Holy Sacrifice**, falls ten weeks later, commemorating the sacrifice Abraham was required to make of his son Isaac. Wealthier families will sacrifice a ram or a goat, and outside the city you will see flocks of livestock being driven into the villages for sale in the markets. If you are touring Turkey and are squeamish, this is a good time to stay away from the villages!

There is a strict protocol concerning the distribution of the meat among relatives and the poor, in keeping with one of the five pillars of Islam – giving alms to the needy. Once the meat has been correctly distributed, there is a huge feast, followed by even more visiting of friends and relatives.

Art and Tradition

Before the foundation of the Turkish Republic in 1923, Islamic art was strictly confined to disciplines such as **calligraphy**, **architecture**, **ceramics** and **glass-blowing**. Any images of people and animals are forbidden, so Islamic art is strong on beautiful geometric design, flowers and nature, moons and stars.

Textiles

If Turkey is famous for anything, it is **carpets**, which range from basic, factory-produced **kilims** to exquisite, hand-woven rugs. Many of the designs are **Kurdish** in origin, depicting scenes from village life. Turkey has a strong fashion design industry, too; international designer **Rifat Ozbek** is just one famous name.

Ceramics

Brilliant blue **Iznik** tiles are famous throughout the world. Intricate tile designs appear in mosques, palaces, fountains, Turkish baths and public buildings and, while the export of antiques is strictly forbidden, there are plenty of quality modern versions on sale in Istanbul, particularly from the **Kütahya** area.

Painting

Turkey did not have much of a painting culture before 1923, although miniature war scenes were very popular among the **Ottomans**. A selection is displayed in the **Topkapı Palace**. The 20th century, however, saw an explosion of artistic talent and Istanbul has several galleries displaying the work of local artists.

Below: *Many hours of painstaking work go into the making of a carpet.*

Calligraphy

Although the majority of visitors won't understand the
intricate calligraphy depicted on tiles and old buildings,
the sheer skill of the craftsmen makes it worth visiting
places like the **Museum of Turkish and Islamic Arts**.

The Performing Arts

Istanbul is Turkey's performing arts capital, with world-
class opera, ballet, symphony and chamber music. The
most common type of Turkish music you will hear is
cheerful village **folk** tunes, played on guitars and wind
instruments. There are home-grown pop artistes, though
none of them is famous outside Turkey.

Istanbul, fast becoming cultural capital of the Middle
East, has a spectacular festival season lasting from March
right up until mid-July. March kicks off with the **International Istanbul Film Festival**, showing a broad
selection of international and Turkish films and now
rated as one of the big-league film events worldwide.
May and June bring the **Theatre Festival**, with dozens
of plays performed in the language of their country of
origin before international audiences. Many of the plays
take place in the beautiful setting of the **Rumeli Hisarı
Fortress**, a 15th-century fortress near the wealthy suburb
of Bebek, with an open-air theatre within the walls.

The biggest event, which takes place from mid-June
to the end of July, is the **International Istanbul Festival**.

Below: *Street theatre is a
common sight in Istanbul,
especially in summer.*

Performances take place
from the entire spectrum
of the arts, including opera,
ballet, modern dance, jazz,
classical, Turkish music,
rock and chamber music.
Big names and world-
famous orchestras attend
every year and this is a
great time to visit the city,
when the weather is per-
fect and the atmosphere
at its most vibrant.

Sport and Recreation

Watching sport, especially **football**, is a much more popular pastime in Istanbul than actually participating in it. Football is a national obsession and when the big teams like **Galatasaray** are playing, Istanbul's bars and cafés are packed solid. If you prefer to do something

Above: *Any visitor to the city is welcome to take on a local at backgammon.*

active, many of the top hotels have health and fitness clubs, as well as tennis courts and swimming pools, usually restricted to guests.

The **Princes' Islands**, which are located just an hour or so by ferry from Istanbul, are the best place to visit if you are interested in beaches for sunbathing. While the Bosphorus is certainly cleaner than it was, it is not recommended for swimming.

Other popular pastimes for those who prefer something a little less active include **backgammon** and **chess**, both of which while away many an afternoon for Turkish men in particular. If you want a game in a café, you will be made most welcome.

No one should visit Turkey without a trip to the **hamam**, or Turkish bath. There are several public facilities in Istanbul, some of which are more used to tourists than others. All the main hotels have them, as well, although it is much more fun to go to a local place. You will need to take your own toiletries and towel, although wooden clogs are provided to stop people slipping on the marble floors. Men and women always bathe separately and only women offer the scrub and massage in the women's baths. You will have to pay an entrance fee and then another price for the scrub and massage, plus a tip for the attendant.

IN THE HAMAM

The first room of the hamam is the **hot steam room**, where you relax, wind down and allow your pores to open. Next, you progress to a **cooler room** where you will be vigorously scrubbed, to the extent that you can see layers of your skin on the floor, and massaged. Next, the masseuse will wash you down with olive oil soap and douse you with cold water before you retire to the **relaxing room** for a cup of tea or coffee, or even a beer. It sounds brutal but you emerge from the hamam with a spring in your step.

Above: *Kebabs in many different forms are sold on every street corner.*
Below: *Apple tea is a very popular drink in Turkey; why not take some home?*

Food and Drink

Turkish cuisine is rated as one of the three great styles in the world, alongside French and Chinese cuisine. It depends on fresh, locally produced ingredients and is often interestingly spicy and surprisingly delicate.

A typical meal starts with **meze**, a range of small dishes shared at the table. It is all too easy to fill up on these: plates of *hummous* (chick pea dip); smoked aubergine purée; stuffed vine leaves in olive oil; meatballs; beans; garlic yoghurt (a Turkish invention); and miniature, stuffed filo pastries. Watch out for some strange ones if you are squeamish – lamb's brain is a delicacy here.

Main courses are either **meat** or **fish**. **Kebabs** appear everywhere – usually small pieces of lamb grilled on a skewer. Sometimes the meat is marinated and sometimes it is plain fast food, dating back to the nomadic origins of the Turkic people. Fish or chicken may also appear on a kebab, accompanied by a shepherd's **salad** of cucumber, tomato, olives and cubed feta cheese. A

FUN WITH FOOD

Turkish *meze* dishes have some amusing names. ***Hunkar Begendi*** (diced mutton on an aubergine purée) means 'admired by the Sultan', while ***Imam Bayıldı*** (roasted, stuffed aubergines) means 'the Imam fainted', apparently derived from the time when a Muslim priest keeled over in ecstasy when he tasted the dish. There are a couple of misnomers, too. **Albanian liver** has in fact nothing to do with Albania – indeed, Albanians have never heard of it. This deep-fried mutton liver dish originated many years ago in Turkey.

lahmacun is a kind of **pizza**, worth knowing if you are vegetarian. Tasty sourdough bread is served with most meals and kebabs often come on a bed of rice.

If you still have room, **desserts** are rich and sinful. Melt-in-the-mouth baklava, dripping with honey, is a must, if only once, while milk puddings are also very popular, although more of an acquired taste.

Devout Muslims don't drink **alcohol** but it is freely available and, in Istanbul, most hosts will join you in a beer, a rakı or a bottle of Turkish wine. A lot of the wines are very drinkable, the whites usually quite dry and light. In cheaper bars and cafés, however, it is quite common to drink **beer** (Efes, the local brew, is a good lager) and enjoy a **rakı**, the local firewater, with your coffee. Rakı is like Pernod or anis and turns white when water is added. It is as fearsome as it looks.

Turks used to drink coffee as though it was going out of fashion. Turkish coffee is thick, strong and black, sweetened and served in tiny cups. Avoid the sludge at the bottom if you want to keep a straight face. Lemon tea is more popular nowadays, although less so with a meal.

There are several different sorts of restaurant in Istanbul. **Köftecis** serve a variety of meatballs, kebabs and grilled meats and are usually quite basic. **Hazır yemek** is Turkey's answer to fast food, where precooked dishes are kept warm and on display. You pick and choose what you want. These restaurants, or **lokanta**, are reasonably cheap and ideal for lunch when you are in a hurry. They are also a good bet for **vegetarians**.

Istanbul also has a thriving restaurant scene at the upper end of the market. Just about any cuisine in the world is available, from Swiss to Japanese, although many would agree that the very best evenings are to be had on a vine-shaded terrace under the stars, on a balmy night, tucking into the freshest of local ingredients and sipping a glass of chilled Vila Doluca.

EAT SAFELY

Turkish food is usually fresh and tasty but there are a few precautions. Don't drink the **water** in Istanbul – even the locals don't drink it. Bottled water is available everywhere and good hotels use treated water for ice. If eating **street food**, buy something that has been cooked in front of you. At an **outdoor buffet**, steer clear of meat and dairy dishes that have been sitting in the sun – this encourages bacteria. If you buy **fruit** from a street vendor, peel it before eating. Be aware that some of the exotic **juices** on sale from juice vendors in summer can act as a laxative!

Below: *A juice seller is a most welcome sight on a hot summer's day.*

2
Topkapı Palace

The **Topkapı Palace** complex (open 09:00–16:30, closed Tuesdays) is probably the first and the most striking sight on any visitor's list of things to see in Istanbul. It stands on the first hill of seven occupied by the old city, **Saray Burnu**, or Palace Point, overlooking the Bosphorus, the Sea of Marmara and the Golden Horn and sections of the original fortifying **walls** still remain.

Built between 1475 and 1478 by **Mehmet II**, the Conqueror, the palace was the administrative seat of the **Ottoman Empire** and the residence of the **Sultan** for over 400 years. More of a mini-city than a simple palace, Topkapı had everything from schools and kitchens to barracks and meeting rooms, all set around a series of courtyards. Today, it is a huge complex of beautifully preserved rooms, fabulously wealthy **museums** of art, ceramics, religious artefacts and weapons, the haunting beauty of the **harem**, the vast **kitchens** and the shady **gardens**. Allow a good half day for a visit, longer in summer when the palace is busier.

The main highlights to see include the **Imperial Gate**; the **Court of the Janissaries**; the **Church of Ayia Irene**; the **Archaeological Museum** and the **Palace Museum**; the **Court of Divan**; the **Porcelain Museum** in the old kitchens; the **Treasury** and the **Armoury**; the **Harem**; the **Imperial Hall**; and the **Museum of Holy Relics**. When you arrive at the palace, buy tickets for the Harem (open 10:00–16:00) straight away as tours run every half hour on a first-come, first-served basis and are quite often completely sold out by mid-morning.

DON'T MISS

*** The Harem: the gilded cage of the sultan's women.
*** The Treasury: contains exquisite jewels of mind-blowing proportions.
** The Armoury: a rather grisly reminder of battles won and lost.
** Museum of Holy Relics: one of the most sacred areas for Muslims.
* Konyalı Restaurant: lunch in the palace gardens with views of the Bosphorus.

Opposite: *The imposing entrance to the magnificent Topkapı Palace.*

IMPERIAL GATE

Also known as Bab-i-Hümayün or **Hangman's Gate**, this is the main entrance to the Palace. The remains of anyone executed by the Sultan would be displayed here as an example to others. Above the gate is the emblem of **Mahmut II**, the last sultan to have lived in the palace.

Just through the gate is the First Court, or the **Court of the Janissaries**, a shady, flower-filled garden where merchants, traders and Janissaries were permitted to mingle freely, as do visitors today. The Second Court was not open to the public. To the left is the church of **Ayia Irene**, the Church of the Divine Peace, built around the same time as Aya Sofya in the 4th century. The church is only open during the Istanbul Festival each summer, when it is used for classical concerts. Next to it is the former Ottoman Mint.

Towards the entrance to the Second Court and the ticket booths is the **Executioner's Fountain**, where the palace gardeners had the grisly task of cleaning their swords after executing those politicians who had displeased the

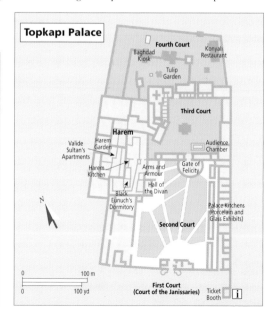

Topkapı Palace

Fourth Court
Baghdad Kiosk
Konyalı Restaurant
Tulip Garden
Third Court
Harem
Valide Sultan's Apartments
Harem Garden
Audience Chamber
Harem Kitchen
Arms and Armour
Gate of Felicity
Hall of the Divan
Black Eunuch's Dormitory
Second Court
Palace Kitchens (Porcelain and Glass Exhibits)
N
0   100 m
0   100 yd
First Court (Court of the Janissaries)
Ticket Booth

Sultan. The pointed towers on either side of the Bab-üs-Selâm, or **Second Gate**, were used as dungeons for those destined for the Executioner's Fountain.

THE SECOND COURT
Porcelain Collections ★★

To the right of the court-yard are the old **Palace Kitchens**, at one point catering for between 2000

Above: *Original tiles from Iznik, in brilliant shades of blue, are priceless today.*

and 5000 people every day. Today, the kitchens house the third largest collection of porcelain in the world, ranging from **Ming** dynasty plates and vases to European glassware, Ottoman silver and 19th- and 20th-century exhibits.

The first two chambers exhibit **Chinese** and **Japanese** porcelain; cabinet after cabinet of priceless urns, plates and jugs, some items gilded with Japanese scenes. Look out for the green **celadon** pieces; these are reputed to have changed colour if touched by poisoned food. Some 12,000 pieces altogether were collected here between the 13th and 19th centuries and over 4500 are on display today. Further on is an array of beautiful **Bohemian** crystal, some of it with gold edging, as well as silver ships, samovars, carved trays and intricate writing chests. Many items are imprinted with the Sultan's monogram, while others were gifts from visiting European diplomats.

In the **Turkish Glass and Porcelain Hall**, look out for the candy-striped, hand-blown glass, which came in 1845 from a factory in the grounds of the Yıldız Palace and is worth millions of dollars. Several exotic perfume flasks are on display in this area, as well as beautiful opaline glassware and some truly hideous vases.

The final room has been kept as a kitchen and is where sweet fruit **sherberts** were made in summer. Enormous cauldrons have been left in place, making it very easy to imagine the scale on which the palace cooks had to work.

IZNIK TILES

Iznik tiles originated in the 15th century, when Mehmet I brought hundreds of **Persian potters** to Iznik, a small town southeast of Istanbul, to produce tiles for his palaces and mosques. The potters were highly skilled and the tiles they produced prized throughout the world, intricately decorated and coloured with a copper blue that was previously unseen outside Persia.

There were once over 300 kilns in the little town, producing tiles for the entire Ottoman Empire. Production ended in the 16th century when an **earthquake** destroyed many of the kilns and workshops, and it was not deemed practical to start again from scratch.

Above: As can be seen from this miniature model, Topkapı is a sprawling complex which takes at least half a day to see.

The Armoury **

Also off the Second Court is the **Armoury**, a collection of over 400 weapons from the 7th to the 20th centuries, among them evil-looking swords, scimitars, complicated rifles, clumsy suits of armour and later, more elegant chain-mail suits. Mehmet the Conqueror's **sword** is also on display.

Just to the south of the Armoury is the **Court of the Divan**, or the council chambers – three rooms under high, domed ceilings where the grand vizier would meet his cabinet to discuss government policy. The Sultan would listen to the proceedings through a grille, banging on it if he wanted to comment on what was being discussed.

The Harem

Whatever raunchy images the word 'harem' conjures up are totally misguided. Harem in Arabic actually means '**forbidden**' but this should be interpreted as meaning 'forbidden to visitors'; the 400-odd rooms of the harem, a few of which are open today, are simply the private apartments of the sultan's wives, concubines, children and the eunuchs who waited on them.

There was a strict pecking order among the 400 residents of the harem. First in line was the sultan's mother, the **sultan valide**, followed by his four official wives, or later, concubines, when sultans stopped bothering with marriage. Being a lady in waiting to the sultan's concubines and their children, or to the sultan valide or the sultan himself was considered a privilege.

Most of the women in the harem were foreigners, either prisoners of war or girls sold into the slave trade by their impoverished parents. The **Caucaus** to the north was a most popular source, as it was known for its beautiful women. Most of the girls were Christians when they arrived but were schooled in Islam in the harem, as well as culture, music, art, deportment, reading and writing and dress. While it was not a life of freedom, it was certainly a privileged existence and as there were no laws of ascendancy, the competition was fierce to bear a son who might ascend the throne. The mother would then become sultan valide, a position which held tremendous power.

The women of the harem were closely guarded by an army of 100 black **eunuchs**; eunuchs for obvious reasons, and black in case one of them slipped through the net and fathered a child. The eunuchs were castrated slaves brought from **Sudan** and while, like the women of the harem, they led a life in captivity, they did have considerable power. The head eunuch ranked only below the sultan, the grand vizier and the minister of religious affairs and was often highly skilled at stirring up rivalry between the residents of the harem.

THE REIGN OF THE WOMEN

The period between 1566 and 1652 is generally referred to as the reign of the women, when a series of powerful women took control over the palace from the harem while their drunken and dissolute spouses and sons idled away their time. Power was keenly contested between the sultan's mother and his first wife. Principal players included **Nur Banu**, **Safiye** and **Kösem**. External affairs during this period were dealt with by a series of exceptionally able grand viziers, while the women mastered the arts of palace intrigue.

TOUR OF THE HAREM

The tour of the harem begins at the **tradesmen's entrance**. Food from the kitchens would have been left on the marble benches here for the eunuchs. Look out for the beautiful green and yellow Iznik tiles in the **Hall of the Fountain**, which leads onto a corridor passing the quarters of the eunuchs. The first main court is the **Court of the Concubines**, around which the four wives or favourite concubines of the sultan had their quarters. They each had their own personal eunuch slaves and ladies in waiting. Much grander is the **Court of the Sultan Valide**, a hall adorned with exquisite French and Italian frescoes of countryside scenes.

Below: *Much of the harem's interior is adorned with exquisite tiles.*

The Sultan's Bath, or **hamam**, is spectacular, adorned in cooling marble and alabaster. The hamam is in fact a series of rooms, one cooler, with underfloor heating, the next lukewarm, where the sultan would be massaged and the hottest, for sweating and scrubbing, situated by the furnace. The Turks consider languishing in a bathtub to be unclean, although there is a rather impressive swimming pool within the harem. The sultan's mother and the four wives or concubines had their own private hamams, too, although the lower ranking women had to share a communal one.

One of the most impressive rooms is the **Imperial Hall**, where the sultan would be entertained, sitting on a gilded **chaise longue**. His mother would sit in the centre of the audience, the wives or concubines on one side and the ladies of the harem on the other to watch the belly dancing and the musicians. The musicians would be blindfolded, as they were in the innermost sanctum of the harem. Note the cobalt blue and coral red Iznik tiles in this and surrounding rooms; the colours come from materials too expensive to use naturally today, and a single tile is worth as much as US$20,000.

Right next door is the **Fruit Room**, decorated with lacquered wood panels depicting fruits and flowers, dating to 1705, when Sultan Ahmet III was in power. The sultan apparently had rather a poor appetite and the **fruit pictures** were to encourage him to eat.

Below: *The sultans enjoyed rooms with elaborate walls but few furnishings.*

The tour progresses to the **Room with Fountains**, which, strangely, is not part of the hamam. The sultan **Murat III** used this as a bedroom and a room in which to receive members of the family and would turn on the taps around the walls to stop unwanted ears from overhearing his conversations.

The last main room is the **Veliaht Dairesi**, or the Crown Prince's Room, with intricate stained glass and a leather-domed ceiling. The crown prince would be kept virtual prisoner in this room to protect him from potential assassins while he was schooled in the ways of the harem. Mercifully, the room has an early form of air conditioning – small fountains in the windows, over which cooling air would blow when the windows were open.

Above: Many of the rooms in the harem have high, domed ceilings.

THE GILDED CAGE

The sultans were determined to eradicate all sources of power except their own. **Mehmet the Conqueror** instituted the tradition whereby all the brothers of a sultan were executed upon his succession and, because the Ottomans did not observe primogeniture, the death of a sultan often resulted in a fratricidal bloodfest. However, **Ahmet I** (1603–17) preferred to place his brother under house arrest in a splendid suite, the **Veliaht Dairesi**, within the harem. From then on all crown princes were subject to *kafes hayatı* (cage life) until the 19th century. Being kept in isolation and ignorant of statecraft meant that most were unfit to rule when they emerged from the cage.

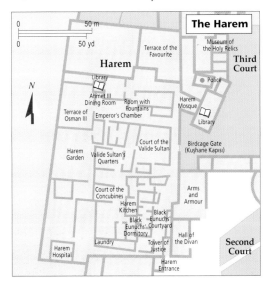

The Harem

0 — 50 m
0 — 50 yd

N

Harem

Third Court

Terrace of the Favourite

Museum of the Holy Relics

Library

Ahmet III Dining Room

Room with Fountains

Police

Harem Mosque

Terrace of Osman III

Emperor's Chamber

Library

Harem Garden

Valide Sultan's Quarters

Court of the Valide Sultan

Birdcage Gate (Kuşhane Kapısı)

Court of the Concubines

Arms and Armour

Harem Kitchen

Black Eunuchs' Courtyard

Black Eunuchs' Dormitory

Hall of the Divan

Second Court

Harem Hospital

Laundry

Tower of Justice

Harem Entrance

Above: *The Gate of Felicity was also known as the Gate of the White Eunuchs.*

THE THIRD COURT

The harem tour leaves you in the third courtyard, the main entrance to which is the Bab-üs-Saade, or **Gate of Felicity**, also known as the Gate of the White Eunuchs. Very few people were received in the third court and the lucky few were received in the **Arz Odasi**, or Audience Chamber, where they would be presented to the sultan by the white eunuchs who guarded this part of the palace. The sultan would recline on a jewel-encrusted divan and only address the visitor via the **grand vizier** – even a foreign ambassador was not considered of enough rank to speak direct to the ruler.

The Treasury ★★★

Near the Audience Chamber is the **Seferliler Quarter**, once a school for boys being trained for state duty and now home to a display of clothing belonging to sultans through the ages, including kaftans, embroidered jackets, magnificent turbans and scarves. The highlight of this area is the **Treasury**, an opulent display of jewels, war spoils and lavish gifts. As you wander from cabinet to cabinet, the jewels seem to get bigger and more incredible. Look for the **Topkapı Dagger**, inlaid with three massive emeralds and the object of Peter Ustinov's desire in the movie *Topkapı*, and the 86-carat **Spoonmaker's Diamond**, the fifth largest in the world. This vast rock is surrounded by several smaller diamonds, further increasing its value. There are giant emerald pendants, jewelled brooches, glittering crests, mother of pearl snuff boxes and even a gold-plated 18th-century baby's cradle.

Museum of the Holy Relics ★

More sombre but nonetheless impressive is the **Museum of Holy Relics**, of particular importance to Muslim visitors. Here resides the cloak of the prophet **Mohammed**, as well as fragments from the prophet's beard, one of his teeth, dust from his tomb, one of his footprints and his sword. It is important to observe correct behaviour in this museum and to dress conservatively.

The Fourth Court

This is the area of the palace filled with beautiful gardens, terraces and fountains, often with tantalizing views across the **Sea of Marmara**. The sultan would stand on these terraces during Ramazan and wait for the sun to set, signifying the end of the day's fast.

You can visit several of the summer pavilions here. The **Revan Köşkü** (kiosk) was built by Sultan Murat IV (1623–40) to celebrate the capture of the Armenian city of Erivan from Persia in 1635, while the **Baghdad Kiosk** followed in 1638 – as its name implies, celebrating the capture of Baghdad. Both have beautiful Iznik tiles on the walls and warm, inlaid wood, as well as spectacular views across the Bosphorus.

Other interesting sights in the Fourth Court include the beautifully tiled **Circumcision Room**, where nine- and ten-year-old boys were circumcised during their initiation into manhood, and also the **Chamber of the Chief Physician**, as well as the 18th-century villa known as the **Kiosk of Kara Mustafa Paşa**. Finally, don't miss the **Mecidiye Pavillion**, which has a stunning marble patio that nowadays houses the panoramic (and very popular) **Konyalı** restaurant.

MANUSCRIPTS OF MINIATURES

The former **Hall of the Treasury** houses one of the palace's only painting exhibits, the Manuscripts of Miniatures. Paintings were rare before the 20th century because the Koran forbade the use of human images in art and most painters during the Ottoman times preferred calligraphy. A few subversive artists in the 16th century, however, did miniature paintings, depicting life under the sultans. Everything from belly dancing and country pursuits to Janissary troops in battle is depicted here on canvases small enough to be hidden in the pages of books.

Below: *With views like this, it's not surprising that the Konyalı restaurant is a popular lunch spot.*

3
Sultanahmet

Just outside the Topkapı Palace is **Sultanahmet**, an area packed with historical interest from all three of Istanbul's great eras: the Byzantine, the Ottoman and the Republican. At one end of the huge square, which in Roman times was a **hippodrome**, are the dusky red domes of **Aya Sofya**, one of the greatest archaeological achievements of its time with its amazing, pillar-free interior and stunning gold mosaics. The magnificent **Blue Mosque** dominates the opposite end of the square, surrounded by six graceful minarets and providing a moment of respite from a rather hectic sightseeing experience.

Close to the Blue Mosque is the 16th-century **Paşa Palace**, today housing the award-winning **Museum of Turkish and Islamic Arts**, a fabulous collection of Islamic artefacts from the 8th century to the present. In contrast, a visit to this area is not complete without heading underground to the impressive **Basilica Cistern**, another spectacular feat of engineering. The small Mosaic Museum is well worth seeing, as is the **Turkish Handicrafts Centre** – a working exhibition of traditional Turkish arts and crafts.

Needless to say, all these wonderful sights in such close proximity mean the area is packed with coach parties in spring, summer and autumn, in turn attracting a thriving souvenir business. Restaurants and cafés, including the famous **Pudding Shop**, line the surrounding streets and while the endless pestering from children and salesmen can be tiring, it is usually good-natured. No one could claim this part of Istanbul lacks atmosphere.

DON'T MISS

*** Aya Sofya: one of the greatest Christian and Islamic monuments in the world.
*** The Blue Mosque: the azure tiled interior is spectacular.
** The Grand Bazaar: thousands of bargains under one roof – but watch out for the tourist traps.
* Underground cistern: a marvellous miracle of ancient engineering.
* The Carpet and Kelim Museum: exquisite rugs and carpets you won't be taking home with you.

Opposite: *Some hotels in Sultanahmet enjoy striking views of the Bosphorus.*

THE HIPPODROME

In Byzantine times, the whole of Sultanahmet Square was a hippodrome, where sports, games, meetings, festivals and mutinies took place. There is nothing to see of the race track itself today as it is some 5m (16ft) underground, but three huge **obelisks** tell something of the region's history.

The actual chariot track was constructed in AD203 by **Septimus Severus** and was shaped like a horseshoe. **Chariot racing** took place for centuries although the area fell into decline when the royal family moved out of the Grand Palace and the crusaders invaded the city in the 13th century. These crusaders stole four magnificent bronze horse statues which used to sit in front of the emperor's box. Today, these statues can be seen in St Mark's Cathedral in Venice.

By the 16th century, the square's fortunes were changing. For years, it had been used as a military training ground but the construction of the **Ibrahim Paşa Palace** added a certain degree of glamour and by the 17th century, when the impressive **Sultan Ahmet Mosque** complex was at last complete, Sultanahmet was virtually surrounded by grand mansions. Prestigious though it may have been, the area had a bloody history, too. In 1826, Sultan Mahmut II carried out the mass slaughter of the unruly **Janissary Corps** here, while the riots of 1909 caused the downfall of Abdülhamid II. Today, the square itself is usually packed with visitors while the side streets are lined with cafés, restaurants and souvenir stalls.

The Obelisks *

The three great obelisks of Sultanahmet are well worth a look before venturing into the main attractions of the square. The **Egyptian Obelisk** is the most striking, carved in Egypt in around 1450BC and erected in Thebes, where it stood in front of the Temple of Luxor. At 26m (85ft) high, the obelisk must have been quite a heavy load to carry to Constantinople, one of the achievements of Emperor Theodosius I in AD390.

The original obelisk is covered in Egyptian **hieroglyphics** but Theodosius had it mounted on marble blocks,

Above: *The Egyptian Obelisk was brought all the way from Luxor.*

carved on all four sides with flattering images of himself and his wife engaged in everyday activities such as watching chariot races and preparing to crown the winner. The centuries have worn the marble almost smooth in places, although the original Egyptian carvings are still sharp and clear.

Close to the Egyptian Obelisk is the **Serpentine Column**, composed of three intertwined snakes carved by the ancient **Greeks** to commemorate their victory over the Persians. The original monument stood in front of the Temple of Apollo in Delphi, until Constantine had it brought to Constantinople around AD330. The serpents' heads were broken off in the 18th century, although one of them was later found and is now housed in the **Archeological Museum**.

The third obelisk, situated at the southern end of the square, is of unknown origin, although it was adorned in brass and bronze by Emperor Constantine VII in the 10th century. The crusaders stole the bronze plaques in 1204, believing them to be gold.

KNOW YOUR KEBABS

Döner: slices carved from a turning spit, served with bread and tomatoes
Köfte: lamb meatballs, grilled and served with bread
Iskender: slices of döner on flat bread with a rich tomato sauce and hot butter on top
Adana: a spicy patty cooked on a flat spit over a grill, served with bread and salad
Testi: pieces of chicken or lamb cooked with mushrooms and onions in a clay pot, which is broken at the table
Beyti: a patty rolled in bread and sliced, usually with garlic, bulghar wheat and yoghurt

Above: *The Aya Sofya has one of the largest domes in the world.*

AYA SOFYA

This magnificent church turned mosque turned museum (open 09:00–16:00, closed Mondays) is one of Istanbul's greatest sights, a vast, brooding cluster of domes built from pinkish red stone, and surrounded by four minarets. Given the period in which it was built, the construction of Aya Sofya is nothing short of an architectural miracle. Only St Paul's in London, St Peter's in Rome and Milan Cathedral are bigger and the sheer size of the dome, 65m (213ft) high by 43m (141ft) wide, defies belief. (In fact, it also defies the laws of physics and the undulating floor of the gallery now has to be supported from underneath by pillars and buttresses in case of earthquakes.) When you enter via the enormous **Imperial Door**, the soaring heights of the dome, resting on two half domes, the giant wooden discs of Islamic calligraphy suspended from the gallery and the huge chandeliers are breathtaking, made all the more atmospheric by shafts of sunlight piercing the gloom.

DIVAN YOLU

Divan Yolu is the main thoroughfare through the old city, running due west from the Hippodrome all the way to the crumbling walls. It was originally laid out by Roman engineers to link up to the main roads across the Roman Empire. Its **milestone**, the Milion, from which all important distances were measured, is close to Yerabatan Saray.

You could spend a whole day wandering along Divan Yolu and still not see everything. The road passes all sorts of **historic buildings**: imperial tombs, the Grand Bazaar, the Press Museum, numerous mosques and even an ancient hamam.

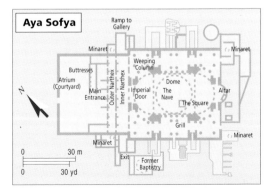

Aya Sofya was built in AD360 by the Roman Emperor **Constantius**. It was burned down in 404 and rebuilt in 415. The church burned down again during the Nika rebellion of 532 and was rebuilt for a second time by Emperor **Justinian** in 537. There are two areas to visit: the main basilica and the gallery. Both are adorned with exquisite mosaics, each tile dipped in gold, and frescoes, although many of the religious images were plastered over during the **iconoclastic** period of the 8th century. Mehmet the Conqueror declared the church a mosque in 1453, while Atatürk pronounced it a museum in 1935.

Outside the museum, various Byzantine relics from around the city adorn the courtyard. There is a fountain for Muslims to wash in before praying and a small house in which the astronomer used to live. His job was to calculate the exact time at which the faithful should be called to prayer. To the left of the main door is the former **baptistry**, later converted into a tomb for the sultans Mustafa and Ibrahim, while several other tombs are located behind it. The four **minarets** were added at various periods from 1453 to 1574, which explains why they are all slightly different.

Through the main entrance is a dazzling 10th-century mosaic of **Madonna and Child**, with Constantine offering the Madonna the city of Constantinople on one side and Justinian proffering Aya Sofya on the other.

To get to the **gallery** (open 09:00–15:30), climb up the steep spiral ramp, which is just wide enough to accommodate a horse-drawn carriage. When Aya Sofya was a mosque, this was the section for women. The small stones protruding from the walls up here are primitive seismographs – a glass would be balanced on the stone to give early warning of earth tremors.

THE EVIL EMPRESS

One of the **mosaics** in Aya Sofya is of Jesus blessing the Emperor Constantine Monomachos IX, watched by his wife Zoe (1028–50). Zoe was, in fact, a suspicious character whose first two husbands died mysteriously, believed to be poisoned. As the mosaic was created during the lifetime of Zoe's first husband, she simply had his face replaced by that of her second spouse, and the same again when she married Constantine, who outlived her.

Below: *The structure of Aya Sofya appears to defy the laws of physics.*

The gallery is where the best mosaics are preserved, many of them portraits of the Byzantine emperors. The most dramatic is the 14th-century **Deesis** at the southern end, depicting Christ, the Virgin Mary and John the Baptist. The mosaics are carefully placed at angles to deflect the light and a rich purple dye, made from sea snails, depicts royalty. Look **Jesus** in the eye and walk past the mosaic; his glance follows you wherever you go.

Downstairs, ignoring the masses of scaffolding, look up at the half-plastered mosaics of the **Archangels Michael** and **Gabriel**, Mary and Jesus. The giant Islamic discs were added when the church became a mosque, bearing the names of Allah, Mohammed and the names of the Caliphs and the Imams of the mosque. The solid marble urns were gifts from Egypt, while the capitals on the columns bear the insignia of Justinian. The muezzin's loge, a later addition, is located in the apse, facing Mecca, while the gilded loge for the Sultan was added in the 19th century. Look out, too, for the **Weeping Column**, a pillar to the left of the Imperial Door which rests on part of an earlier structure. The earlier part of the column is cooler than the rest and gathers dew, which was believed to have mystical powers. Emperor Justinian is said to have touched the column in the belief that it would cure his migraines.

Below: *Many of Aya Sofya's original mosaics have survived, despite being plastered over by the iconoclasts.*

THE BLUE MOSQUE

The Blue Mosque (open from before dawn prayers to after dusk prayers; closed during services), or Sultan Ahmet Mosque, was built for the young Sultan Ahmet I (1591–1618) to rival Aya Sofya in grandeur. At the time, it was the only mosque in the world apart from El Haram at **Mecca** to have six minarets, and is still unique in Istanbul in this respect. A seventh minaret has since been added to the mosque in Mecca.

While the huge central dome, supported on four columns, is less ambitious architecturally than Aya Sofya, the exterior of the Blue Mosque has an extraordinarily graceful wave effect. The main dome, 23.5m (77ft) across, is surrounded by four smaller ones, in turn encircled by countless even smaller domes, while still more domes crown the walls of the enclosed courtyard. There are stunning views of the whole structure from an outer courtyard, where people gather before a service to gossip. The shady inner courtyard has an ablutions fountain at its centre, while the walls and domes create shade for study or quiet contemplation. Because of the sheer volume of worshippers that attend the mosque, the ritual washing today takes place at a row of taps along the northern outside wall.

Above: *The Blue Mosque is the only one in Istanbul to have six minarets.*

CALL OF THE MUEZZIN

Before the age of electronic speakers, the haunting call to prayer of the **muezzin**, who would climb to the top of his minaret, would echo out across Istanbul's rooftops five times a day, making an almost musical sound. All **mosques** summon the faithful through an often tinny speaker nowadays, however, and if there is one right outside your bedroom window, you are unlikely to sleep through the dawn call. While they all stick to almost the same schedule, one is often a minute or two behind the next, so the crackling wail can go on for some time.

Right: *Sultan Ahmet I is interred in a tomb on the northern side of the Blue Mosque.*

BACK IN TIME

Every mosque in Istanbul originally had a *muvakkithane*, or **horologist**, housed in a separate building alongside the mosque. These horologists had many functions. Their prime purpose was to use **sundials** and **mechanical clocks** to calculate the exact times of prayer, five times a day, and the dates of Ramazan. They also developed a skill at predicting **meteorological** phenomena such as hot and cold spells and even storms, and were surprisingly accurate. In the days when most people didn't have watches, they were also a convenient place for passers-by to stop in and find out the time.

But as sundials began to lose their importance and mechanical clocks spread, the *muvakkithane* began to fade away and only 30 remain in Istanbul today.

Visitors, however, must enter through the **north gate**, and not at prayer times, when up to 25,000 people are packed into the vast space. You must dress modestly and hand over your shoes to an attendant. Women must cover their heads. Inside, the scene is breathtaking. Brilliant light pours in through the high, stained-glass windows, drawing out the cobalt blue of hundreds of thousands of blue 16th-century **Iznik** tiles that line the walls and the domes. Huge **kilims** are scattered across the stone floor, while glass lanterns are strung between the four vast columns that support the huge dome.

There is little furniture inside any mosque. Noteworthy examples in the Blue Mosque are the lattice marble imperial **loge** on the left, the marble pulpit and the beautiful raised chair from which the teacher, or **imam**, gives his sermon. Outside, various smaller buildings make up the whole complex. There is an old primary **school** and a soup kitchen, or **imaret**, where the poor would come to be fed. Until the 19th century, there was also a hospital, the only one to be constructed in Istanbul in the 17th century, and a **caravanserai**, where visiting travellers could stay. The sultan's old mansion, **Hünkâr Kasri**, houses a collection of carpets and kilims from 200 mosques around Turkey. On the northern side is the **tomb**, or türbe, of Sultan Ahmet I (open 09:30–16:30 Wednesday–Sunday), decorated with 17th-century tiles. The sultan, his wife, three sons and sundry other relatives are buried in sarcophagi, draped with dark green fabric to symbolize the religion of Islam.

PAŞA PALACE

Close to Sultanahmet is the 16th-century **Paşa Palace**, built in 1524. The palace was a gift from Süleyman the Magnificent to his close friend, son-in-law and Grand Vizier Ibrahim Paşa. Paşa, however, was a victim of palace politics. Süleyman had him **executed** in the Topkapı Palace in 1536, suspecting him of disloyalty. Nevertheless, the Paşa Palace retained his name. In 1983 it was renovated and today houses the **Museum of Turkish and Islamic Arts** (open 10:00–17:00 Tuesday–Sunday). The museum was awarded prizes by the EC in 1984 and UNESCO in 1985 for its collection and contemporary display techniques.

The museum houses everything from carpets and manuscripts to stone, ceramics, calligraphy and wood, everything reflecting daily life in Turkey from the 8th to the 19th century. There is an informative video presentation on the first floor, giving a crash course in Turkish history and a wonderfully peaceful old Turkish coffee house in the grounds, where traditional coffee is brewed over an open fire, or on a hot day, where you can sample a sweet fruit sherbet.

Among the displays themselves, don't miss the historic **manuscripts**, the Turkish **miniatures** and the **calligraphy**. There is a whole section on Ottoman artefacts and a collection of sultans' **monograms**, or tugra. In the ethnographic collection there is a beautiful display of wall-hung **kilims** and carpets, complete with wool-dyeing and weaving techniques.

CAFÉ SOCIETY

Turkey is famous for its **coffee** but ironically, coffee is far less popular than **tea** nowadays because the cost of importing it from Brazil is so high. If you do come across it, drink it sweet in a tiny cup and leave the gritty residue at the end. Most people in cafés drink tea, in a straight glass with no milk. **Apple tea** is a local speciality and worth a try, although the granule version is somewhat less appealing to many. If you really need a coffee fix and cannot stomach the strong stuff, ask for Nescafé.

Left: *Black tea and backgammon are archetypal Turkish images. A game of backgammon is a great way to get to know the locals – just turn up at any bar or café. Language need not be a barrier.*

YEREBATAN SARAY

The 'sunken palace' (open 09:00–17:30) faces the Aya Sofya, marked by a stone pillar rising from a small square at ground level. In fact, it is not a palace at all, but a spectacular and slightly spooky underground **cistern**, also known as the Basilica Cistern. Built in the 6th century by Emperor Justinian the Great, this was just one of a network of 18 cisterns under the city, creating a vast underground waterway.

This particular cistern is 70m (230ft) wide by 140m (460ft) in length and can hold a staggering 80,000m³ (2,825,120ft³) of water, or as Justinian liked to put it, a fleet of 16 **warships**. The volume of water was considered enough to sustain this area of the city for a considerable length of time during a siege.

The domed roof is supported by 336 columns, some of them salvaged from ruined buildings around the city. Two are of particular interest, with **Medusa** heads as bases. The cistern still works today and is full of water,

which was originally pumped from a reservoir 19km (11.5 miles) away in the direction of the Black Sea along a line of aqueducts. The modern presentation of the cistern is, however, quite different from the original, with piped classical music and coloured lights for effect. Visitors walk along a series of walkways. This is one of Istanbul's attractions that children can also enjoy, particularly as a reward for trailing round the mosques and palaces of the area.

Left: *Some exhibits in the Mosaic Museum date back to AD500.*
Opposite: *The underground cistern is flooded with coloured light to enhance its dramatic effect.*

Mosaic Museum *

The mosaics in this museum were discovered in the 1950s when archaeologists on a Turkish-Scottish team were excavating behind the Blue Mosque. A mosaic **pavement**, dating back to AD500 was uncovered, rich with scenes from mythology and country pursuits such as riding and hunting. The pavement, it transpired, was part of a route leading from the emperor's palace, where the Blue Mosque now stands, to the harbour.

Further mosaics were located under a row of shops called the **Arasta**, which today house souvenir vendors and cafés, as well as the entrance to the museum.

Haseki Hürrem Hamam *

Just to the east of Aya Sofya is a former **hamam**, or Turkish bath, built in 1556. Originally, this was designed as a twin hamam with separate sides for men and women, each side with the three rooms for disrobing, washing and sweating and massage. The men's side is considerably more ornate than the women's, with inlaid marble and stained-glass windows.

Today, the hamam houses the **Turkish Handwoven Carpet Centre** (open 09:30–17:00 Wednesday–Monday), run by the Ministry of Culture and selling lovely original motif carpets, all of them woollen and all hand-dyed. This is a good place to buy a carpet; the prices are more honest than in some of the shops of the Grand Bazaar and the quality is high.

CARPET SCAMS

These scams seem pretty obvious, but it is all too easy to be pressurized into buying a carpet you didn't want and getting ripped off.

Beware of anyone who says they have a **friend** or **relative** with a carpet shop; they are simply a salesman on commission. In the carpet shop, beware the words '**old**', '**Persian**', '**rare**' and '**silk**'. Silk may well turn out to be mercerized wool; hand made may turn out to be churned out on a machine. If you are going to be spending a lot of money, shop around very carefully.

Never let the vendor **ship** your carpet home for you. The worst case is that is won't arrive at all; second worse is that what arrives won't be what you paid for. If you need the carpet shipped, buy it wrapped and **ship it yourself**.

Right: *The Grand Bazaar is massive, and it is therefore easy to get lost here.*

KAPALI ÇARŞI

Kapalı Çarşı, also known as the Covered Market or **Grand Bazaar** (open 09:00–19:00, closed Sundays), is one of Istanbul's famous landmarks, a staggering 4400 shops and stalls under one roof. The bazaar was founded immediately after the conquest of Istanbul in 1453, when a roof was built over a small gathering of traders. The market expanded as caravanserais (travellers' lodges) were added to its outskirts, so that **merchants** from distant trade routes could set up shop here. Despite ten fires and two **earthquakes**, the bazaar retains much of its original atmosphere and the original core still stands.

Locals and tourists shop at Kapalı Çarşı, although as a tourist you have to be in the right frame of mind as the pressure from the stallholders to buy is intense. There is no point going when you are tired or stressed! Everything imaginable is on sale here: leather jackets and bags; designer fakes; onyx statuettes and chess sets; brassware; copperware; gold and silver jewellery; rolls of silk fabric; slippers and bridal gowns; antiques and, of course, carpets. The goods are displayed in a kind of massive Aladdin's Cave, piled high in a sepia half-light, pierced by the occasional shaft of sunlight from one of the high, side windows.

The market is a short walk from Sultanahmet. Head along the main road Divan Yolu and turn right into Vesirhani Caddesi. Pass by a large, Ottoman Baroque mosque from the 17th century, the Nurousmaniye Mosque. The other side of the mosque, on Çarşıkapı Sokak, is one of the main entrances to the bazaar.

This entrance leads onto the main street of the bazaar, **Kalpakçılarbaşı Caddesi**, a busy alleyway packed with jewellers' shops. It is a good idea to keep this in mind as a landmark, as all the smaller streets radiate off this one and once you are lost, you may as well be in a maze.

The jewellers' stores sell gold by the gram and will charge extra for workmanship. As with anything in the bazaar, it is really a personal decision as to whether you have found a bargain. The chances are it won't be of great value as the place is essentially a tourist trap but then, it could be something you would never find at home.

As in the old days, trades tend to be grouped together, which makes shopping for a particular item easier. Off Kalpakçılarbaşı Caddesi is Sandal Bedesteni, a 16th-century corner of the bazaar which has been restored and is now used for **carpet auctions**. It is here that the original structure of the bazaar, with domed ceilings, is best preserved. In the very centre of the building is Cevahir Bedesten, the original, 15th-century core of the complex, while to the right of the main 'street' is the **Furrier's Market**, the only two-storey area, now packed with **leatherware** and fake designer clothes. Beware of the money traders; many of them are **black marketeers** and you may well be ripped off, particularly given the massive wad of lire you will get for your dollar or pound.

ISTANBUL'S HANS

Hans are inns built hundreds of years ago for nomadic traders. Most of them are concentrated in the narrow streets around the **Grand Bazaar**; they are two-storey buildings where the **traders** would spend the night, keep their animals and also store their goods.

At the turn of the last century, when camel caravans were replaced by trains and the inns were no longer needed, the hans were taken over by **artisans**, who needed to be close to the Grand Bazaar. Goldsmiths, silversmiths, tanners, weavers, and other craftsmen still occupy the buildings today and you will see whole streets around the bazaar dedicated to one type of trade. The area is fascinating to stroll around.

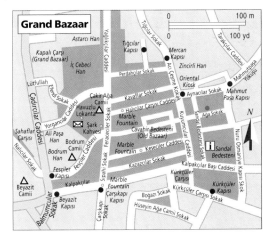

4
West of the Old City

Istanbul has a wealth of less-visited sites to the west of the **Old City**, extending as far as the magnificent 4th-century **walls** and beyond. Some of the neighbourhoods may be a little scruffy but a day of zigzagging around by taxi, dolmuş, ferry and on foot will reveal exquisite mosques, like the **Rüstem Paşa Camii** (mosque) and impressive monuments like **Yedikule Hisarı**, the magnificent **Fortress of the Seven Towers**. Tour coaches may be few and far between in these areas but you will pass through some fascinating old residential districts.

There are several major sites to visit, too. Don't miss the colourful **Egyptian Bazaar** at **Eminönü**, where a variety of spices, nuts, seeds, fruits and herbs are sold from huge sacks, or the two great mosques of **Süleyman** and **Fatih**, piercing the hilly skyline with their lovely slender minarets. Take a trip to **St Saviour in Chora**, first a church, then a mosque, now a museum containing some of the most important religious mosaics and frescoes in the world. Walk along the line of the old **city walls**, where some of the huge gates and fortifications have been preserved.

Take a trip, too, along the **Golden Horn** to the district of **Eyüp**, one of the world's most important sites for Muslims with its beautiful mosque and the tomb of Eyüp Ensari, standard-bearer and close friend of the prophet **Mohammed**. Once you have explored the mosque complex, relax under the trees at the **Café Pierre Loti** on top of the hill as old Istanbul and the Golden Horn stretch out in front of you.

DON'T MISS

*** Chora Church: some of the world's most beautiful mosaics and frescoes.
*** Eyüp Mosque: one of the holiest sites in the Islamic world.
** Spice Bazaar: a veritable feast for the senses and the perfect place to shop for gifts with a difference.
** Old city walls: Istanbul as it was centuries ago.

Opposite: *Elaborate mosques are dotted all over the city, giving Istanbul, particularly the old part, a unique and much photographed skyline.*

TURKISH DELIGHT

Turkish Delight was invented by **Ali Muhiddin**, a confectioner who moved to Istanbul from the Black Sea area in the late 18th century. Candies at the time were rock hard, so he decided to try something chewy instead and came up with *rahat lokum*, meaning 'comfortable morsel', which soon became, simply, *lokum*.

Lokum became very popular with the sultans, and the confectioner developed **new flavours**, among them walnuts, pistachios, orange, almonds and rose water. His old shop is still owned by his descendants and is situated on Hamidiye Caddesi in Eminönü.

EMINÖNÜ

Eminönü is one of those districts that sums up everything about Istanbul. The steps of the Yeni Mosque are a popular meeting place and are packed in the late afternoons, drenched with golden sunlight, people soaking up the atmosphere, buying fruit juice from the many vendors, meeting friends and enjoying the view of the water where the Golden Horn flows into the Bosphorus. The square in front of the mosque, facing the **Galata Bridge**, is also packed as buses drop off their cargo and locals struggle home, laden with goods from the nearby Spice Bazaar.

Across the road from here, rows of **fishermen** line the waterfront, surrounded by buckets containing their catch, while ever-hopeful cats weave in and out of their legs. Crowds mill around on the quay, waiting for the ferries in order to cross over to Asia or to the Princes' Islands and, with the ever-present din of the traffic and the different smells of street food cooking, there is a constant buzz of activity.

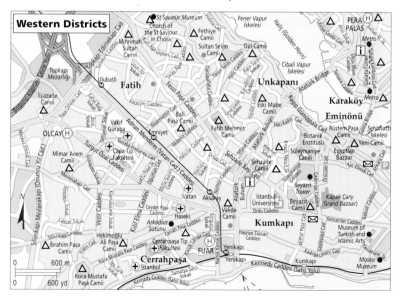

Yeni Camii *

Commissioned by the sultan valide **Safiye Sultan** in 1591 and completed several generations later by Hatice Turhan Sultan, mother of **Mehmet IV**, the Yeni Camii is a typical design of cascading domes and elegant minarets. Inside are beautiful tiled walls adorned with gold, and marble fittings. The same sultan valide built the Egyptian Bazaar.

Egyptian Bazaar ***

Also known as Mısır Çarşısı or the **Spice Bazaar**, this covered market was built at the same time as the Yeni Camii and got its name from the high volume of Egyptian goods that were sold here. Today, it is vibrant and colourful and if you prefer more quirky souvenirs, almost better than the Grand Bazaar for shopping.

Above: *A wide variety of spices can be obtained at bargain prices in the Egyptian Bazaar.*

Spices and condiments are piled high at every stall: buckets of nuts, sunflower and pumpkin seeds by the sackload, dates, figs and apricots, cumin, cardamom, coriander, great vats of green henna and mountains of sticky nougat. Turkish delight is available in every imaginable flavour, from rosewater to mint and nut, while huge, dripping honeycombs beckon those with a sweet tooth. At some stalls, contraband Iranian **caviar** is on sale at astonishingly low prices. Little packets of Iranian **saffron**, supposedly the best in the world, also make great gifts for keen cooks. Some of the herb concoctions are decidedly suspect, particularly those marked rather coyly '**Turkish Viagra**' and 'Sultan's love potion'. Sample these at your peril.

Further into the bazaar, bolts of fabric, shoes and household goods are on sale. The vendors are more laid-back than those in the Grand Bazaar and you will be invited to sample goods with no pressure to buy. People still haggle in here, but less aggressively.

OLD BOOK BAZAAR

If you leave the Grand Bazaar via the Haci Husnu Kapısı gate and cross the street, you will see the Old Book Bazaar, or **Sahaflar Çarşısı**, a collection of shops dating from Byzantine times, selling old books, engravings and maps. Some of the books are old, although not valuable antiques, and some merely second hand, but you can find interesting English-language material about aspects of Istanbul. Of added interest is that many of the stallholders are members of the rare **Halveti Dervish order**, although you won't see them performing their whirling dances here.

Rüstem Paşa Camii *

A short walk from the Egyptian Bazaar northwest along Hasır-cılar Caddesi is another pretty mosque, Rüstem Paşa Camii. The walk itself is an added bonus as it goes along one of Istanbul's most colourful local shopping streets, lined with fruit and vegetable vendors and stores selling household goods. The mosque itself was built in 1561 and is adorned from one end to the other with Iznik tiles, many of them depicting beautiful flowers. The entrance is above street level as the ground floor originally consisted of shops, installed to finance the mosque.

Above: *The Süleyman Mosque is the city's largest after the Blue Mosque.*

Süleymaniye Camii **

A couple of blocks behind Eminönü but unmissable because of its vast size is the Süleyman Mosque, the city's second largest mosque. This spectacular structure, its domes piled up like a giant plate of meringues, sits on top of one of the old city's seven hills and can be seen from miles away in every direction.

The mosque was built between 1550 and 1557 by Süleyman I, 'The Magnificent' and was designed by the architect **Mimar Sinan**, one of the greatest of the Ottoman era. Inside, the building is surprisingly simple, with Iznik tiles decorating the *mihrab* and light shining down through beautiful stained-glass windows.

Typically, the mosque complex is like a small town with a caravanserai, hamam, soup kitchen, school and a shopping arcade which today is full of souvenir shops and snack bars. There are some rather elaborate **tombs**, too, of Süleyman, his daughter and his favourite wife, the evil **Hürrem Sultan**.

CITY WALLS

Istanbul's impressive walls were built in the 5th century by the Emperor Theodosius II and stretched all the way from the **Sea of Marmara** to the **Golden Horn**, enclosing the peninsula occupied by the old city on the land side. More walls remain along the Sea of Marmara. Most of the city's defences were destroyed during the **Ottoman invasion** and by the 19th century, the walls were quite severely neglected. Many of the towers and bastions were delicately restored in preparation for the 500th anniversary of the invasion and have since been declared a Cultural Heritage Zone by **UNESCO**. But great chunks of the walls are mere crumbling, mossy remains. You can admire what is left by wandering inland from the upper reaches of the Golden Horn.

The land walls were triple strength, so to speak, with a main wall and a frontal wall separated by a deep trench. Several gates were built at the points where the roads entered the city, their names denoting the name of each road's ultimate destination. If you take a taxi along the Golden Horn to just before the **Fatih Köprüsü Bridge** and turn inland on foot, there are good views of the end of the land walls from the front of the Ivaz Efendi Camii (mosque).

It is possible to wend your way along much of the ruined wall down in the direction of the Sea of Marmara. Several of the neighbourhoods are run down, the magnificent palaces of the distant past long since destroyed, but the occasional glimpse of a huge gate or an ancient tomb makes the journey worth your while.

SINAN THE ARCHITECT

The architect of the golden age of the Ottoman Empire was **Mimar Sinan** (c1497–1588), an Anatolian caught up in the *devşirme*, the annual levy of Christian boys taken to become slaves of the state. After service as a military engineer in the **Janissary Corps** he was appointed Chief of the Imperial Architects in 1538, a post he held for the next 50 years. He is officially credited with 323 structures, including mosques, mausoleums, hospitals, palaces and public baths. Of these, 84 are still standing in Istanbul. Sinan was 65 when he completed the **Süleymaniye**, the crowning glory of Ottoman architecture in Istanbul, and is buried in a mausoleum in its shadows.

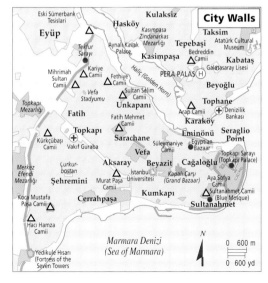

AQUEDUCT OF VALENS

Stretching across the road known as Şehzadebaşı Caddesi is the spectacular **Bozdoğan Kemeri**, or Aqueduct of Valens, a two-storey aqueduct believed to date back to the **Emperor Valens**, who ruled from AD364–378. It served a vital role in transporting water across the city and was repaired in 1019 and many more times subsequent to this when it was damaged by battles and earthquakes. The aqueduct collapsed partly after neglect during the era of Süleyman the Magnificent but restoration work began again in the 1980s.

Below: *Every wall and ceiling at Chora Church is covered with works of art.*

CHURCH OF ST SAVIOUR IN CHORA

Located just inside the land walls near Edirne Kapı gate, St Saviour in Chora, or **Kariye Camii** (open 09:30–16:00, closed Wednesdays), is one of the most amazing religious buildings in Istanbul, thanks to its fabulous mosaics and beautiful **frescoes**. Some of the art within the church is regarded as the most significant in the Christian world and it is well worth the detour from the main sightseeing spots.

You can easily walk to Chora, which means 'in the countryside', alongside the walls from the Golden Horn. The houses around the church have been beautifully restored and there is the usual collection of souvenir stalls and snack restaurants.

The original building, constructed in the 4th century, was outside the then city walls attached to a monastery, hence the name. When the main walls were built 100 years later by **Theodosius II**, the fortifications went around the monastery, although it kept its name.

By the 11th century, the monastery was in ruins but the church was restored. The frescoes were painted around 1320 by **Theodore Metokhites** and, despite a fair amount of abuse over the centuries, are in astonishingly good condition today. In the 16th century, the church was turned into a mosque and all the frescoes plastered over. Luckily, they were successfully re-exposed in 1874

Left: *Intricate Biblical scenes are beautifully depicted at the Church of St Saviour in Chora.*

by a Greek architect named **Kuppas**. In 1948 the building was officially designated a museum and the final stages of the fresco-cleaning completed.

There are more than 100 mosaics and frescoes in the museum, in two separate areas. The main section of the church is decorated with mosaics. The inner and outer narthex are adorned with a series of dedicatory **mosaic** panels showing St Peter and St Paul and Christ with his mother. Metokhites himself is also pictured, offering Chora to Jesus.

Images of Jesus' lineage are depicted on the northern and southern domes of the main hall, while beautiful, intricate mosaics of the life of the Virgin Mary adorn the first three sections of the inner hall. A big mural in the outer narthex shows scenes from Jesus' infancy, including the visit from the **Three Wise Men**, while the domed vaults in the same area show amazingly well preserved pictures of Jesus' ministry and religious leadership.

Finally, three breathtaking panels in the nave show the **assumption** of the Virgin Mary, with Christ standing behind her holding her soul, represented as a baby. They are surrounded by apostles and early bishops of the church and watched over by six angels.

The frescoes are in the parecclesion, an aisle to the side of the church. This was built to house various tombs and the frescoes show scenes of death and **resurrection**. Among the most notable are a picture of Jesus breaking the gates of Hell and raising Adam and Eve from their tombs and an image of the Day of Judgement.

GLOSSARY
Bab • Gate
Bedesten • Grand Bazaar
Caddesi • Avenue
Camii • Mosque
Hamam • Public bath
Harem • Section of the palace reserved for women
Imam • Muslim priest
Han • Artisans' workshop
Kervansaray • Large inn for putting up camel caravans
Meydan • Square
Saray • Palace
Sokak • Street
Türbe • The tomb of an important person
Yalı • Seaside mansion

Right: *The tomb of Mehmet the Conqueror is at the Fatih Camii.*
Opposite: *The Yedikule Fortress Musuem is set into the massive land walls.*

FATIH CAMII

Heading back in the direction of Sultanahmet along Fevzi Paşa Caddesi is the impressive Fatih Camii, the city's first large mosque complex, built by Mehmet the Conqueror. In Ottoman times, the main street here was lined with noblemen's homes, although the former grandeur of the area hardly shows today.

Mehmet the Conqueror built his mosque on top of a hill in 1470 in typical grand style. The complex contained eight schools, a library, a hospital, various caravanserais, a hamam and fountains. In its time, it was the most important cultural centre of the city. But like much of Istanbul, the mosque was toppled by a huge **earthquake** in 1766. It was completely rebuilt a year later in Baroque style.

While the outside is impressive, there is not much to look at inside. Don't miss the tomb of **Mehmet the Conqueror** in front of the *mihrab*, rebuilt in 1784 after the earthquake in the same Baroque style as the mosque. Mehmet's wife Gülbuhar Sultan is buried next to him.

YEDIKULE HISARI

Right at the opposite end of the land walls, where the fortifications meet the Sea of Marmara, is the massive **Fortress of the Seven Towers**, or Yedikule Hisarı (open 09:30–16:30, closed Mondays). Originally built as an outpost to the city and later used to guard the treasury, and then as a dungeon, the fortress is open to visitors today, although it is quite a distance from the main tourist sights. The fortress is visible from the main road coming in from the airport and is often the first thrilling glimpse of ancient Istanbul for visitors.

The Byzantine emperor would enter the city via **Altın Kapı**, or the Golden Gate, a triumphal arch built in the 4th century by Theodosius I. Theodosius II later incorporated this gold-plated door into the walls and built four of the seven towers. The Golden Gate, use of which was reserved for the Emperor, led to the city's main road, the Mese, which ended in front of Aya Sofya

---

FOUNTAINS OF LIFE

Water is critically important to the Muslims because of the many rituals of ablutions; for everybody to wash five times a day, a lot of water is needed. As a result, fountains and taps are built in mosques, streets and large residences, sometimes carefully hidden. **Fountains** are often quite elaborate, particularly the indoor kind, which may be designed to create a soothing sound, or to flow down past a window, thus forming instant air conditioning.

church. The fortress itself was completed by Mehmet the Conqueror, who added three more towers to create an enclosed fortification to protect the **Treasury**. This was later moved to the Topkapı Palace.

Yedikule had a new use under the Ottomans – as a **dungeon**. Foreign ambassadors from enemy states as well as Ottoman statesmen were imprisoned here, many of them meeting a gruesome end. The fortress was used as a **prison** right up until 1831, after which time it found a new use as a **gunpowder factory**. The structure was awarded museum status in 1895 and restored in 1959. Today, you can visit some of the towers and admire the walls. For more atmosphere, try to attend one of the open-air concerts which take place here in summer.

EYÜP MOSQUE

Eyüp is regarded by Muslims as one of the holiest sites in the world after Mecca, Jerusalem and Medina. The community is quite a long trip up the Golden Horn from the main tourist area, well beyond the Fatih Köprüsü Bridge. You can take a ferry from Eminönü, or a taxi.

Eyüp is where Eyüp Ensari, standard-bearer and close friend of the prophet Mohammed is buried. The cemetery here is still considered a burial place for the privileged and many **sultans**, prime ministers and important political figures are laid to rest here.

Eyüp was killed in the first Arab siege of the city, between 668 and 669 but his tomb was only discovered several hundred years later by Aksemseddin, teacher to Mehmet the Conqueror. The mosque was built by Mehmet after the conquest of Istanbul, using the finest tiles and calligraphy available. Once again, the massive earthquake of 1766 razed an important monument to the ground and the

---

PASSAGE TO MANHOOD

In Turkey, boys are circumcised when they are eight to ten years old, marking their passage into the Muslim faith and manhood. The day of **circumcision** is a big event, in which the boy is dressed in a special white suit with a red satin sash and visits friends and relatives before being paraded around the neighbourhood in great ceremony. Nowadays, the ritual often includes a visit to the **Eyüp Mosque** to pray.

After the operation, the family feasts and parties late into the night, while friends and relatives bring **gifts** to the boy, now recovering in bed, to commemorate the occasion.

mosque was rebuilt in 1800 by **Sultan Selim III**. The new version, like the original, is particularly beautiful, with blue Iznik tiles, gold leaf interiors, sumptuous carpets and exquisite chandeliers.

Eyüp's **tomb**, which survived the earthquake, is just as lavishly furnished, with gold and silver, crystal and more tiles. Muslims seeking miracles have made pilgrimages here for centuries, filing past the 'wishing window', a grille that opens onto the mosque's inner courtyard. Families, too, bring their young sons here, dressed in smart white uniforms with a red sash and a red cap. The boys are on their way to their ritual **circumcision** and have come here to pray beforehand. They come here partly because of the holiness of the site and partly because Eyüp was famous for his great love of children. This is also the reason, according to local legend, for the proliferation of **toy-makers** in the Eyüp area, although they can no longer be seen today.

Do remember that this is a very holy site and dress respectfully; women must have their heads, shoulders and upper arms covered and shorts are frowned upon. Friday is not a good day to visit, as the mosque is then packed with worshippers.

Above: *A kebab is an inexpensive and tasty snack and is ideal as a meal on the move.*
Opposite: *Ablutions must be performed before prayer, five times a day.*

Pierre Loti Café *

Stroll up the steep hill to the north of the mosque through the cemetery (a good chance to admire the elaborate headstones) to the café made famous by Frenchman Pierre Loti. The café has beautiful **views** over the Golden Horn and is where Loti is said to have come for the inspiration for his novels. The café is in a pleasant area of narrow streets; like the rest of the Eyüp district, you will find kebab stalls, yoghurt vendors, juice vendors and little shops selling religious souvenirs.

ROMANCE IN EYÜP

Frenchman **Pierre Loti** (1850–1923), whose real name was **Louis-Marie Julien Viaud**, was a celebrated **novelist** at the same time as serving in the French navy. His romantic novels incorporate intricate details of daily life in the Istanbul with which he fell in love.

Loti lived in Eyüp and had an illicit affair with a married Turkish woman, to whom he dedicated one of his novels, *Aziyadé*. When he eventually returned to France, she vanished mysteriously before she could join him there. The **café** named after him near the Eyüp Mosque is where he is said to have come for his inspiration.

5
Modern Istanbul

Istanbul's commercial centre, **Beyoğlu**, lies on the north shore of the Golden Horn, linked to the old city by the **Galata Bridge**. Immediately across the bridge, the city clings to a steep slope, topped by the **Galata Tower**, while **Karaköy**, the area around the foot of the hill, leads to the city's passenger shipping terminal, where luxury cruise ships moor up, adding a touch of glamour. Beyond here, past the ferry terminal, lavish European-style **palaces** line the shores of the Bosphorus, overlooked by ranks of five-star hotels. Up on the hill, known as **Pera**, banks, foreign consulates and commercial offices are clustered in the tangle of streets around **Taksim Square**, where all Istanbul's busiest roads and bus routes converge.

Beyoğlu has been settled as long as the Old City has been inhabited, although for years it was a poor relation of walled Constantinople, a motley gathering of foreigners, non-Muslims, hopeful traders, immigrants and later, slums. At the same time, new ideas were tried here, including electricity and the **Tünel**, Istanbul's first underground train. The area reached its heyday in the 19th century, as grand embassy buildings and diplomats' houses were built along the crest of Pera Hill and the sultans developed a taste for their European palaces on the shores of the Bosphorus over Topkapı. The glamour faded somewhat in the 20th century as the embassies were downgraded to consulates when the capital moved to Ankara. But while Beyoğlu could do with a lick of paint, there are several interesting **museums** to visit as well as some excellent **shopping** and great **nightlife**.

DON'T MISS

*** Dolmabahçe Palace: the opulent Ottoman palace where Atatürk once lived.
** Çiçek Pasajı: enjoy your dinner where the locals eat, in the buzzing market, or Flower Passage.
** Naval Museum: see the royal barges once used by the Sultans.
* Yıldız Palace and Park: open space and attractive pavilions at Istanbul's most popular park.
* Pera Palas: afternoon tea at the hotel once frequented by Agatha Christie.

Opposite: *Narrow residential streets on the northern shore of the Golden Horn.*

Above: *The fishermen are out on Galata Bridge, come rain or shine.*

KARAKÖY

Also known as **Galata**, this is the former banking and commercial centre which grew up when the Byzantine emperors and Ottoman sultans banished European entre-preneurs to ply their trade outside the city walls. By the 13th century, it was virtually autonomous as a **Genoese** colony and has re-mained distinctly **European**, with **Armenian** and **Greek** churches alongside mosques. The name Galata either comes from the Gauls who invaded the area in AD237, or from the Italian *calata*, meaning 'the slope leading down to the harbour'.

The Genoese enjoyed special commercial privileges throughout the 14th and 15th centuries and the area became a hotbed of **foreign trade**. Several large banks and shipping companies still maintain offices here and in between the modern blocks are found scruffy little

WHIRLING DERVISHES

The whirling dervishes were a **religious order** founded in the early 13th century. Through chanting, prayer, music and a strange, whirling dance, clad in black capes, conical hats and swirling, flowing white robes, they believed they could enter a trance and get closer to God.

Dervishes were, however, deeply **conservative** and were banned in the early days of the Turkish Republic. Today, they exist as a **cultural** organization rather than a recognized religion and perform on the last Sunday of every month at the former Whirling Dervish Hall in **Galata**, which is now the calligraphy museum.

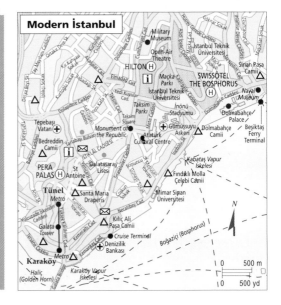

alleyways consisting of hardware stores; it is not unusual to find an entire street selling air conditioning units or water filters from hole-in-the-wall shops.

The **Galata Bridge** from Eminönü to Karaköy was opened in 1992 and was built to replace an iron pontoon bridge of 1912. It is one of the busiest stretches of road in the city and opens up to allow large ships into the **Golden Horn**. Summer and winter, rain or shine, you will see scores of fishermen lined up along the bridge, lines cast into the murky waters of the Bosphorus.

Galata Tower **

Dominating the Karaköy skyline, the round **Galata Tower** (open 09:00–21:00, except the restaurant which is open till late) has stood here in one form or another since AD528, when the first wooden **defence** tower was erected. A structure resembling the present one was built by the **Genoese** in 1349 as part of their city walls but has changed shape often since then, particularly during the Ottoman era, when it burned down several times. Apartment buildings now stand in place of the old city walls that once adjoined the tower while the pointed roof was rebuilt in 1964.

The tower has had various uses. During the reign of Sultan Murat IV it was a launch pad for Hezarfen Ahmet Çelebi, an early **hang glider**, who jumped off the top and was carried by sea breezes all the way across the Bosphorus to the Asian side. There is a copper etching of his effort next to the elevator on the ground floor.

The tower was a **prison** during the time of Süleyman the Magnificent and later the home of the Ottoman military band. After World War I it was used as a lighthouse. Today it is a tourist attraction, with shops, cafés, a revolving restaurant and a Turkish nightclub inside.

Below: *The Galata Tower stands out prominently from the city's skyline.*

Taksim Square *

Passing through the chaos of **Taksim Square** is an inevitability of a trip to Istanbul, as all the main roads in the new city meet here and it is the drop-off point for the airport bus and many of the bus and dolmuş routes. It is also a good point of reference if you are new to the city.

The word 'Taksim' actually means 'distribution point' and the name comes from a network of water **conduits** that originally met here, laid under the rule of Sultan Mahmut I in the 18th century.

While the square itself is not particularly attractive, there are several interesting sights around it. The monolithic, fifties-style building to the east is the **Atatürk Cultural Centre**, home to many events during the Istanbul Festival every summer. At the western end is Cumhuriyet Anıtı, the **Monument of the Republic**, which was sculpted by the Italian Pietro Canonica in 1928. One side of the monument depicts the War of Independence and the other side represents the Republic of Turkey. **Atatürk** and other Turkish leaders are featured on the monument.

ISTIKLÂL CADDESI

Formerly the somewhat grand-sounding **Grand rue de Pera**, Istiklâl Caddesi, or Avenue of Independence, is one of the few streets in the new city where it is pleasant to walk. The street is mainly, but not completely, pedes-trianized, and trams run along its length, along the spine of the hill from Taksim Square to **Tünel Square**. Off to the sides are dusty little alleys, often strung with washing and noisy with children playing – in other words, a typical inner-city Istanbul scene.

Left: *Cumhuriyet Anıtı is an important monument on Taksim Square.*
Opposite: *Most of the tourist spots feature belly dancing performances.*

There are plenty of interesting buildings along the main street. Starting at Taksim Square, look out for the **French Consulate** on the right, a former hospital used to treat plague victims in 1760. Further down, on the left, is **Galatasaray Square** with its famous **Lycée**, one of the city's oldest schools. When the school was opened by Sultan Abdülaziz in 1868, it was a great status symbol as boys could learn there in Turkish and **French**. On the same side of the road, four or five buildings on, is St Antoine Italyan Katolik Kilisesi, Istanbul's only **Catholic** church and a fine example of neo-Gothic architecture.

Still on the left are two more interesting churches. Santa Maria Draperis is a **Franciscan** church, built in 1789, while down the first left turn from there is Istanbul's largest Protestant church, the **Crimean Memorial Church**, built in 1868. Look out, too, for the consulates, particularly the Dutch, the Russian, the Italian and the Swedish, all housed in elegant mansions, built when Pera was the height of fashion.

Istiklâl Caddesi ends at Tünel Square, where Istanbul's earliest **metro** emerges. This has to be one of the shortest underground lines in the world at just 550m (600yd) and with only two stops. Built in 1874, the Tünel connects Karaköy with Beyoğlu and was built to save the rich European merchants the trouble of walking up the hill from the banking quarter in Galata to their mansions in Pera.

NINETEENTH-CENTURY PROSPERITY

Towards the middle of the 19th century, Constantinople's social and economic life moved to **Pera**, an area long established as the city's European quarter. The commercial hub revolved around the multinational banks and the stock exchange, buttressed by luxurious shopping arcades and elegant hotels lining the boulevards. The great European powers, hustling for territory, trade and influence in the Middle East, built magnificent embassies and private residences, owned mainly by foreigners, reflecting the era's wealth and taste. The westernized Turkish elite did not gravitate towards Pera until the turn of the century.

Above: *Turkish baths are incredibly ornate and a session at a hamam should last several hours.*

Below: *Çiçek Pasajı is a taste of the 'real' Istanbul, a must for a noisy dinner.*

Galatasaray Hamam **

If you want to try a Turkish bath and have no objection to venturing further afield than your hotel, the **Galatasaray Hamam** is one of the best, as well as being one of the kindest to tourists. It is located on Turnacıbaşı Sokak, just before Galatasaray Square, off Istiklâl Caddesi. The baths date back to the 15th century and are luxurious inside, with high marble ceilings and private cubicles in which to rest. Naturally, there are separate sections for men and women.

Çiçek Pasajı ***

To the right of Istiklâl Caddesi, just before Galatasaray, is the **flower passage**, or Çiçek Pasajı, a must for a taste of local life. The passage is in fact a kind of covered courtyard, belonging to the **Cite de Pera**, a 19th-century shopping arcade that epitomized Pera's growth as a modern European-style city. Originally, people would sit at upended beer barrels topped with marble slabs but the tables were made more permanent in the 1980s after the building had to be renovated. Today, it is packed with drinkers and diners eating at countless tiny, crowded restaurants, each one blending into the next.

CELEBS AT THE PERA PALAS

Kings, presidents and movie stars have chosen the Pera Palas throughout its history, although its glamour now is somewhat faded. The guest list includes:
• Agatha Christie
• King Edward VIII
• Mata Hari
• Sarah Bernhardt
• Greta Garbo
• Zsa Zsa Gabor
• Jacqueline Kennedy Onassis
• Julio Iglesias

The atmosphere is great, buzzing with Turkish and foreign voices, and although prices have been loaded somewhat for the tourists, Çiçek Pasajı is still a very 'local' place to hang out. Most of the food consists of **meze** and **kebabs**, washed down with beer and rakı. Street entertainers, belly dancers and musicians wander around and the area has its fair share of carpet touts, too, although it is all very good-natured. At the end of the passage is the **Galatasaray Fish and Flower Market**.

Pera Palas *

At the end of Piremeci Sokak, a narrow street leading to the right off Istiklâl Caddesi, is the **Pera Palas**, Istanbul's most legendary hotel and a tourist attraction in its own right. It was built in the 1890s by the Belgian businessman Georges Nagelmackers, founder of the **Orient Express**, who wanted somewhere in keeping with the train for his guests to stay when they reached Constantinople.

The hotel evokes a bygone age with its grand salons, its old-fashioned lift and quaint bar. It was believed that **Agatha Christie** stayed here, though this is now in dispute, but **Atatürk** favoured the hotel and his room, 101, has been turned into a museum. Ask at reception for the keys.

AGATHA CHRISTIE

Author of *Murder on the Orient Express*, Agatha Christie is believed to have been a frequent guest at the **Pera Palas**. During one of her stays there, she vanished mysteriously for 11 days. Her whereabouts has never been discovered, although it was believed that a small **key** would hold the answer to her disappearance. After her death, an American psychic, **Tamara Rand**, predicted that the key was in room 411 of the Pera Palas where, sure enough, it turned up. The mystery, however, remains unsolved.

Below: *Agatha Christie and Atatürk were patrons of the Pera Palas Hotel.*

Below: *Conrad is just one of the many five-star hotel groups in Istanbul.*

CONFERENCE VALLEY

Beyond the hustle and bustle of Taksim Square lies the relatively open space that has been dubbed 'Conference Valley' because of its concentration of modern hotels and **conference centres**. Just over a century ago, this area was used for little but the sultans' hunting and country pursuits, particularly in the latter half of the 19th century, when they moved out of Topkapı into the more modern palaces of Dolmabahçe, Çırağan and Yıldız. Broad, tree-lined streets lined with exclusive mansions sprang up, looking down the hill over the **Bosphorus**.

Today, all the best spots are taken by the hotels – the Swissôtel complex, the Conrad and the Hilton, all of which stand out when viewed from the water in a way that the architects of the beautiful palaces might not have wished for. There are also a lot of university buildings in the area, formerly barracks, and some of the city's most fashionable business **restaurants**. Palaces aside, the most interesting sights for visitors are the museums; the **Naval Museum**, the **Military Museum**, the **Dolmabahçe Palace**, the **Yıldız Palace** and the small City Museum. This is also the main crossing point from this side of the Golden Horn to the Asian side of the city, or back to Eminönü. The lively ferry terminal is located between the Dolmabahçe Palace and neighbouring Çırağan Palace and is always packed with holidaymakers, commuters, hawkers and general bustle.

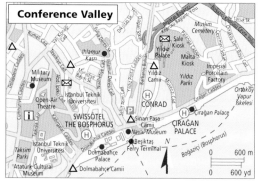

Naval Museum **

The Naval or Maritime Museum (Deniz Müzesi, open 09:00–17:00, closed Wednesdays and Thursdays) is located just behind the Dolmabahçe Palace. You cannot miss it; cannons, anchors and propellors from Turkish **warships** are scattered around on the lawn outside.

Inside is an impressive display of Turkey's military prowess over the centuries, particularly the 16th century, when the Ottoman Empire extended around most of the Mediterranean. Don't miss the kayaks, or **imperial barges**, which were used to ferry the sultans and their harems to and from their palaces along the Bosphorus. Long and narrow, they were propelled by 13 sets of oars and travelled at considerable speeds. The ladies of the harem were coyly hidden in their boats behind elaborate lattice screens.

The museum also contains a statue of **Barbarossa** (1483–1546), the famous privateer who was commissioned by Süleyman the Magnificent to conquer North Africa. He is buried nearby. There are old maps of sea voyages from the 15th century, naval uniforms, artefacts from battles against the **Venetians** in the 16th century and even from the 1974 invasion of Cyprus. Children will enjoy looking at the remains of a German U-boat in the museum gardens. It was sunk in the Black Sea when it hit a mine in World War I and discovered and raised and moved to the museum in 1993.

Above: *Imperial barges were used to ferry the Sultan and his entourage to the river palaces.*

BARBAROSSA

Barbarossa, which means 'red beard', was born on the Greek island of **Lesbos** in the 15th century. He was feared throughout the Mediterranean as a savage **pirate** and for several years terrorized the coast of North Africa. When the area was attacked by Spain, Barbarossa sought the aid of Turkey and helped the Turks in turn make significant acquisitions for the Ottoman Empire. As a reward, he was made a **high admiral** of the Turkish fleet and is buried today in Istanbul.

Military Museum **

Located to the north of Taksim Square on Cumhuriyet Caddesi, the Military Museum (open 09:00–17:00, closed Wednesdays and Thursdays) is located within the military college complex. Numerous weapons, uniforms, battle standards, military artefacts and cannons bearing the monograms of various sultans are all on display. One of the most interesting sights offered by this museum are the luxurious **tents**, which were used as headquarters for the sultans during battle campaigns. They are amazingly elaborate, threaded with silver and gold and heavily embroidered. There is also a whole room devoted to Atatürk, Turkey's most famous general and first president of the new Republic.

The old section of the museum contains more military memorabilia of uniforms, guns, armour and cannons as well as a corner devoted to the collaboration between Turkey and Germany before World War I. One of the most fascinating items on display is a section of the massive **chain** that was stretched across the mouth of the Golden Horn to keep the invading armies out – quite a feat of engineering in its time.

If you are visiting the museum in summer, you should time your excursion for mid-afternoon, when the **Janissary Band** performs between 15:00 and 16:00. This band, one of the world's first military ensembles, would parade through towns and villages in front of the conquering Ottoman army, instilling a suitable level of respect into the new subjects.

KNOW YOUR MEZE

If you cannot see what you want on display, the following are the most popular dishes you are likely to see on a menu:
Pilaki • white beans in vinaigrette
Börek • filled filo pastry
Yaprak dolması • stuffed vine leaves (with rice or lamb)
Kabak dolması • stuffed courgette or marrow
Patlıcan salatası • aubergine purée
Beyaz peynir • white sheep's cheese
Domates salatalık • tomato and cucumber salad

Yıldız Palace and Park *

Located on a hill behind the Çırağan Palace Hotel, Yıldız is the largest park in Istanbul (open 09:00–18:00 daily). It has elaborate coffee shops, gardens and **pavilions** constructed by various sultans, but mainly by Abdülhamid II (1876–1909), who was a master carpenter and spent much of his time here alone. Although the park was restored in the 1980s, it has an air of faded glory today.

The pavilions are known as 'kiosks' and there are several to admire. The Pavilion Kiosk at the top of the park was built in 1870 and has wonderful views. The Winter Garden, a pink and white **pastry shop**, and the Green Nursery, another coffee shop with outdoor seating under the trees, are close by. The Malta Kiosk, used for official receptions by the lonely sultan, has been turned into a restaurant and is surrounded by beautiful trees with stunning views out across the Bosphorus.

While in the park, visit the Yıldız Palace Museum (open 09:30–18:00, closed Mondays), the **carpentry workshop** of Sultan Abdülhamid II. Porcelain, exquisite vases and the sultan's own woodwork are on display. Check out the Şale Köşkü (open 09:30–17:00, closed Mondays and Thursdays) as well, a pretty wooden chalet with 64 rooms, built in 1898 for visiting dignitaries. Abdülhamid lived here himself for a while, preferring the solitude to palace life down on the shores of the Bosphorus.

BEST BUYS

Istanbul is a great place to shop for gifts, clothes, things for the house and quirky food items to take home.
Best buys include:
• Carpets and kilims
• Brassware
• Leather bags
• Onyx chess sets
• Gold and silver jewellery
• Turkish delight
• Caviar
• Saffron
• Herbs and spices
• Ceramic tiles (but don't try to buy antiques)

Opposite: *Interesting war memorabilia from several centuries is on display at the Military Museum.*
Below: *Yıldız Palace, home of Abdülhamid II, is located in Istanbul's largest park.*

Dolmabahçe Palace ★★★

The lavish Dolmabahçe Palace (open 09:00–16:00, closed Mondays and Thursdays) is built on a piece of reclaimed land (*dolma bahçe* means 'filled in garden') on the shores of the Bosphorus, just in front of the area that is dubbed 'Conference Valley'. The palace was built in 1854 by Sultan Abdülmecit, who was keen to show the world that the declining Ottoman Empire could move with the times although in fact, the ambitious project of building the palace further plunged the empire into **debt** as considerable sums had to be borrowed.

The palace was constructed in a garden that had previously been the location of earlier sultans' wooden kiosks, all of which had burned down in 1814. Designed by the court architects Nikogos and Karabet **Balyan**, it turned out to be more opulent and over the top than anything the city had seen, 600m (656yd) long with 285 rooms, 43 salons and six long balconies. No expense was spared on the materials inside the palace, with almost indiscriminate use of gold leaf, crystal and marble.

For all the expense that went into it, Dolmabahçe wasn't even used that much. It was the imperial residence of a few of the sultans until Abdülhamid II moved out to Yıldız, after which time it was mostly used for state receptions and ceremonies. Later, **Atatürk** adopted the palace as his home and lived here until his death on 10 November 1938. All the clocks in the palace have been set to 09:05, the exact time of his passing.

Above: *Gold leaf, crystal and marble feature heavily in Dolmabahçe Palace.*
Opposite: *In its day, the palace was the city's most opulent structure.*

Get to Dolmabahçe early, particularly in summer, when there are long queues. You must take a guided tour, which lasts an hour and you may have to wait up to an hour to get in. Flash photography is forbidden inside. The tour encompasses the private and public rooms, including the **harem**. One of the highlights is Muayede Salonu, the dramatic **State Parlour**, two storeys high and adorned with cupolas, arches and columns. A 4.5 ton **chandelier** from Britain, the largest in the world, forms the centrepiece.

Look out, too, for the magnificent staircase leading to the Salon of the Ambassadors. The balustrades are made from **Baccarat crystal** and the ceilings in the main room are decorated with gilded wood.

Everything about this palace is awe-inspiring. Even the *hamam*, the Sultan's bath, is covered with precious alabaster imported from Egypt with everything from the basins to the fountains clad in expensive stone. In the Mavi Salon, everything gleams with gold, from the dining chairs to the ornate ceilings. More modest is the **Pink Salon**, the bedroom and study where Atatürk spent his last days. The rooms have been preserved exactly as they were at the time of the great man's death and a Turkish flag has been draped over his bed.

BREAKFAST

Traditional Turkish breakfast is delicious, consisting of fresh bread, jam, olives, tomatoes, cucumbers and salty white sheep's milk cheese. Tea is a typical breakfast drink (the Turks move onto coffee later in the day), although some people prefer *sıcak süt* – hot, sweetened milk. If you cannot survive without your usual cooked breakfast, boiled eggs are easy enough to find, though bacon is another matter as Turkey is a Muslim country and pork products are not eaten.

6
The Bosphorus

The **Bosphorus** is the lifeblood of Istanbul and a journey along it is by far the best way to appreciate the city. This narrow strait gives the city a sense of perspective. Its cooling breezes sweep away the dust and pollution in summer and the constant to and fro of ships, tankers, ferries and fishing boats gives Istanbul a permanent, moving backdrop, even at night.

Just 32km (20 miles) long and 500m (547yd) wide at its narrowest point, the Bosphorus has shaped Istanbul's history. Jason is said to have sailed along here in search of the **Golden Fleece**, and **Ulysses** is believed to have explored here. Mehmet the Conqueror built two of the most impressive forts at the strait's narrowest point to protect it, while **Russia** has always coveted it. Sitting at one of the waterside cafés watching Russian naval vessels glide by en route to the Middle East is a harsh reminder of the days of the Cold War.

It is hardly surprising that the Bosphorus is one of the world's busiest waterways. Oil tankers from the **Caspian Sea** chug along to the Mediterranean, while commuter vessels bring workers into the city from the wealthy suburbs on the European side, and also carry hordes across from the populous Asian side. Big **cruise ships** line up at the Istanbul passenger port, while tiny fishing boats dart in and out of all the traffic. Navigation is hazardous; the surface current flows towards the Sea of Marmara, while a deeper current at around 40m (130ft) tugs in the opposite direction. In the days before motor boats, vessels had to tow a deep anchor or net to catch this current.

	Black Sea
EUROPE	Bosphorus
	Beykoz
Sarıyer	
Gaziosmanpaşa	ASIA
Beşiktaş	
Üsküdar	Bosphorus

DON'T MISS

** **Çırağan Palace:** opulent Ottoman palace on the Bosphorus, now a luxury hotel.
** **Anadolu Hisarı:** wonderful old fortress in beautiful setting on the Asian side.
** **Ortaköy:** pretty waterfront town with New Age market on Sundays and lively café society.
** **Fishing Villages:** lunch on the freshest fish imaginable by the water.
* **Sadberk Hanım Museum:** an impressive collection of Islamic artefacts housed in a private home.

Opposite: *The graceful Bosphorus Bridge joins Europe and Asia.*

COW CROSSING

The name Bosphorus is said to have come from the Greek, *bous* (cow) and *poros* (crossing), based on an ancient legend. The god **Zeus** had been having an affair with **Io** and in deference to his wife, **Hera**, turned his former lover into a cow. In a vindictive mood, Hera sent a horsefly to sting the cow, which promptly swam across the strait to escape the insect.

An alternative explanation is the Turkish *Boğaziçi*, which means throat or strait (*boğaz*) and inside (*iç*), in other words, 'inside the strait'.

You can explore the Bosphorus by taking a trip on a sightseeing ferry, which sails up to the mouth of the **Black Sea** and back, taking approximately two hours each way. Alternatively, you can zigzag backwards and forwards across the river from the European to the Asian side, taking a day or two. It is possible to drive along the Bosphorus as well, of course, although the magic is lost if you are not right on the water, admiring the beautiful views of the city skyline.

Look out for magnificent **Ottoman palaces**, lovely old wooden villas, pretty little **fishing villages**, waterside mosques and Mehmet the Conqueror's two massive **fortresses**, Rumeli Hisarı and Anadolu Hisarı.

Ferries leave regularly from the dock at Eminönü. Get there early to get a decent seat, bearing in mind your need for sun or shade.

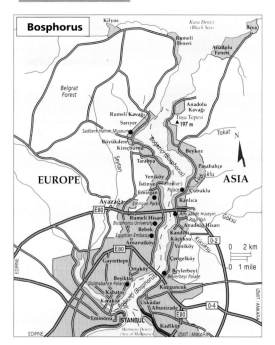

FROM EMINÖNÜ TO THE BOSPHORUS MOUTH

Çirağan Palace *

No sooner has the boat passed the Dolmabahçe Palace and the Naval Museum, another marble fantasy palace looms up on the European shore of the Bosphorus: this is the Çirağan Palace.

Built by the same architect as the Dolmabahçe Palace, this lovely marble residence was constructed for **Sultan Abdülaziz** in the middle of the 19th century. At the time there was already a palace on the site, known as the White Palace, but Abdülaziz had the original one torn down in 1856 to make

Left: *The Çırağan Palace is now a luxury hotel and attracts many high-level international conferences to its opulent rooms.*

way for a new one, also white, just like something out of a fairytale. In the end he did not get very much use out of the palace as it was used as a virtual **prison** for the deranged Sultan Murat V, who stayed here for 27 years after being deposed.

Parliament met at the Çırağan Palace after the 1908 Revolution of the Young Turks but the building was largely destroyed by a raging fire in 1910 and subsequently lay in ruins until the well-known Kempinski hotel group restored it to its former glory in the 1980s, turning it into what is now Istanbul's most luxurious **hotel**. While it is not open to the general public for sightseeing, you can slip through the foyer and turn to the right from the rooms section to see the old palace, which contains suites and banqueting rooms, with many of the original features intact.

Bosphorus Bridge *

Looming up ahead of you is the fifth-longest **suspension bridge** in the world, the graceful Bosphorus Bridge. This bridge not only links Europe with Asia but also forms a vital commuter route into the centre of Istanbul. The bridge was opened in 1973, having taken approximately three years to build, and was inaugurated on the 50th anniversary of the Turkish Republic. It is almost a kilometre in length and the road is 64m (210ft) above the water at its centre.

PERFECT PATISSERIES

Turkish people have a sweet tooth and, in addition to the usual Turkish Delight, almond candies, baklava and nut concoctions, you will see row after row of delicious **chocolates** in some of the city's patisseries. The **Divan Hotel** on Taksim Square has one of the most famous outlets, operating independently from the hotel itself. The shelves are packed with hand-made chocolates, exquisitely decorated cakes and tempting pastries, either to eat there or to take away. If you are feeling particularly extravagant, check out the patisserie at the **Çırağan Palace Hotel**, where praline-filled, moulded sultans' heads make a wonderful gift.

Above: *Ortaköy, with its lovely mosque, is a friendly, multi-racial fishing village.*

Ortaköy ★★★

Ortaköy is a gem on the shores of the Bosphorus, in the shadow of the huge Bosphorus Bridge. The best time to visit is on a Sunday, when there is an outdoor **craft market**, a breath of fresh air after the crowds of the Grand Bazaar. The narrow winding streets are packed with antique shops, jewellery designers, modern interiors shops, fashionable cafés, bars and restaurants. In the main square, you can enjoy a cappuccino and watch the fishing boats, as crowds gather to enjoy the sun and the convivial atmosphere. The market is worth exploring for anything from bits of glass to earrings, scarves, knitwear and New Age trinkets. Best of all is a row of Armenian women in headscarves making fantastic **pancakes** in the open air, with a vast array of delicious fillings.

What is best about Ortaköy is the fact that Greek, Jewish, Armenian and Turkish communities live side by side here in complete harmony. Clustered around the main square in the side streets are a synagogue and a 19th-century Greek Orthodox church and, on the main square, a beautiful **mosque**, built by Balyan for Sultan Abdülmecit in 1855. It has its own quay in front, so the sultan could arrive in his barge and go straight to his pew. The interior is in an ornate Baroque and Rococo style.

Bebek *

Bebek is a wealthy, leafy suburb of Istanbul with a buzzing atmosphere, thanks to the presence of the **Bosphorus University**. It was formerly Robert College, the first American college to be founded outside the USA, built with the backing of philanthropist Christopher R Robert during the Crimean War. The university which occupies the site today is one of Turkey's most prestigious.

Bebek itself is a highly desirable place in which to live, with some impressive houses. You will pass **Hıdiv Sarayı**, a palatial residence on the waterfront that is now the Egyptian Consulate. Slightly further along is **Bebek Camii**, a pretty mosque, with fishing boats moored outside, and also a series of grand mansions, some of them built in the old wooden style.

Rumeli Hisarı **

Just before the Fatih Bridge, the second huge suspension bridge that crosses the Bosphorus at its narrowest point, is Rumeli Hisarı (open 09:30–17:00, closed Mondays). This dramatic, walled **fortress** was built at great speed in just four months in 1452 by Mehmet the Conquerer, with the help of 3000 workers, to dominate the waterway in tandem with Andolu Hisarı on the opposite shore. Once the fortress was complete, Mehmet effectively controlled the Bosphorus and went on to conquer Istanbul.

Since then, the fortress has been used as a barracks and a prison and is now a museum. The original wooden floors remain intact in the upper right-hand tower, while you can see the minaret of the original mosque in the grounds. There is a big **amphitheatre**, used for plays and concerts in summer, particularly during the Istanbul Festival.

> **TURKISH LOOS**
>
> There is a small fee for using a public toilet in Istanbul. These may be of the sitting or squatting variety (the latter is considered more hygienic) and **toilet paper** is not always provided as it is customary here to wash (hence the tap or hosepipe in each cubicle) and use the paper for drying. Take your own paper if you are concerned.
>
> Toilets near the main tourist attractions are usually Western-style and relatively clean. Elsewhere, check first if you are squeamish; loos on ferry boats tend to be particularly unpleasant. If you are really desperate, every **mosque** has a toilet, although the quality cannot be guaranteed.

Below: *Rumeli Hisarı was built by Mehmet the Conqueror in just four months.*

EUROPE
Black Sea
Rumeli Kavağı
Sarıyer
Büyükdere
Anadolu
Kavağı
Sadberk Hanım Museum
Tarabya
Emirgan
Rumeli Hisar
Bosphorus University
Bebek
Ortaköy
ASIA
Üsküdar

TULIPS FROM TURKEY

The reign of Sultan Ahmet III (1703–30) was known as Turkey's **Tulip Period**. Tulips were imported to Turkey from Persia and have grown here for many centuries, long before being exported to Holland. During Ottoman times they were very popular ornamental flowers and growers were richly rewarded for coming up with new strains. The tulip gardens at **Topkapı** provided live entertainment by night, as the palace attendants would fix lighted **candles** to the shells of tortoises which became conditioned to moving towards the tinkle of gold coins thrown into the garden by the sultan. The result was a constantly moving pattern of lights between the flowers.

Opposite: *Anadolu Kavağı is a great lunch stop for fish-lovers.*
Right: *Many of the beautiful old wooden houses, or yalı, on the Bosphorus are still standing.*

FISHING VILLAGES ALONG THE BOSPHORUS

From this point, the scenery is extremely pretty; lush gardens surrounding beautiful old mansions interspersed with picture-postcard fishing villages, their quays lined with tempting-looking restaurants. If you are touring by car, stop at **Emirgan Korusu**, beautiful gardens where there is a spectacular **tulip festival** every May. There are three mansions in the woods: the **Yellow Mansion** is a café, while the **Pink Mansion** is built in the style of a traditional Turkish house and contains a café and a museum of the Bosphorus; the neo-Classical **White Mansion** is used as a concert hall.

Tarabya *

This is one of the most scenic fishing villages, set around a sparkling little cove, a collection of gleaming yachts anchored in the inlet. **Yalıs** and summer residences of many of the consulates are scattered along the shore here, idyllic refuges to which the diplomatic community would retire a century ago (and still do) when the heat and dust of the city got too much. The village was once known as Pharmakeus, or '**Poisoner**', thanks to a legend that Medea threw the poison intended to kill Jason into the water here, although in Byzantine times, the name was changed to **Therapea** because of the curative powers of the hot springs. These were unfortunately destroyed by a massive earthquake in the 14th century.

Sadberk Hanım Museum *

After Tarabya, the Bosphorus begins to widen as the Black Sea looms, with more palatial homes overlooking the glassy water. It is worth paying a brief visit to the Sadberk Hanım Museum (open 10:30–18:00 in summer, 10:30–17:00 in winter, closed Wednesdays), Turkey's first private museum, opened in 1980 by wealthy business-man Vehbi Koç, in memory of his wife Sadberk Hanım. The museum has amassed quite a collection of Islamic and archaeological artefacts and **Ottoman heirlooms**, attract-ively displayed in a pretty wooden summerhouse.

Afterwards, there are some excellent fish restaurants in the town of Sarıyer, which has a lively fish market and makes most of its income from the sea.

Rumeli Kavağı and Anadolu Kavağı **

Rumeli Kavağı is a fishing village, the last stop of the ferry on the European side, right at the mouth of the Bosphorus. You could either get off here for lunch or cross over to the Asian side, to **Anadolu Kavağı**, which is another pleasant lunch spot. The tourist ferries usually stop here for two or three hours, time to have a delicious seafood lunch, enjoy the shade of one of the many tea gardens or pick at fresh mussels from the many **fried mussel** vendors. These two villages used to be the **toll gates** of the Bosphorus and fortifications were built here in the 18th century. Climb up the hill behind Anadolu Kavağı to the medieval Byzantine castle, which has spectacular views out across the Black Sea.

BEACHES

Despite the abundance of water, it is difficult to find a good place to swim near Istanbul as the **Marmara Sea** and **Bosphorus** are heavily polluted. **Black Sea** beaches are cleaner but chilly and there can be a dangerous undercurrent. **Kilyos** is a pop-ular resort on the European side of the Black Sea a half-hour dolmuş ride away from Sarıyer. If you must swim, do so only from designated beaches and never alone.

Above: *The quiet fishing villages on the Bosphorus are a stark contrast to the bustle of Istanbul.*

OPIUM SMUGGLING

Turkey used to supply over half the world's opium, smuggled across Europe to America. The USA eventually pressurized Turkey to clamp down on the opium trade, which it did. **Poppies** are still cultivated but strictly for medicinal purposes. Drug smuggling in Turkey is no joke; if caught, you will endure a very long prison sentence. The film *Midnight Express*, while viciously anti-Turkish, does give one an idea of what can happen to smugglers in Turkey.

ANADOLU KAVAĞI TO EMINÖNÜ

The Asian side of the Bosphorus is less developed than the busy European shores and gives a real glimpse into how life must have been 100 years ago. Coloured fishing boats bob in tiny inlets, while wooden houses and **yalı** in pastel shades sit right on the waterfront. During the week, the pace of life is slow and relaxed, although day trippers flood in at weekends. All along the shores are wonderful fish restaurants, coffee shops and places to sit and watch life go by on the water.

Beykoz *

A former fishing village, Beykoz lost much of its quiet charm at the end of the 19th century, when the area became industrialized with the opening of a large **glass** factory. Glass products from this region are still sold around Istanbul today. There are a number of elegant mansions and yalı along the water and a couple of old streets to look at. The area is known for several different delicacies. The 'koz' in Beykoz means walnut, and nut products are still sold here, although several of the surrounding orchards have been swallowed up by urban sprawl. The **turbot** fishing has quite a reputation in this village, too, should you stop for lunch.

Kanlıca ***

Just to the north of the huge sweep of the Fatih Sultan Bridge, Kanlıca is one of the few Asian villages that has managed to preserve its traditional charms. Stop at one of the coffee houses and try the local **yoghurt**, for which the village is famous. It is served with a spoonful of sugar and is quite delicious. Take some time, too, to wander around the old streets and admire the wonderful wooden yalı along the waterfront, many of which have been beautifully preserved.

Travelling by boat is often the best way to admire the old wooden mansions, which overhang the water. Just after the bridge is a pinkish coloured yalı, the Hekımbaşı Salih Efendi Yalısı, built by **physician** Salih Efendi, who attended sultans Abdülmecit and Abdülhamid in the 19th century. Efendi was famous for the **herbal medicines** he grew in the garden of the yalı and the house remains in the family today.

Just along the shore from here is an ancient-looking building, Amcazade Yalısı, the oldest wooden building still standing in Istanbul today, constructed in the late 17th century by Grand Vizier Amcazade Hüseyin Paşa.

Left: *Don't forget to try the famous yoghurt in Kanlıca, a traditional fishing village on the Asian side of the Bosphorus.*

PIDE PLEASE

Pide is the Turkish equivalent of pizza and is a cheap and staple street food. It can be the saving grace of Turkish cuisine for vegetarians on a budget. Some samples of toppings are:
Kaşarlı: cheese, sometimes with peppers and onions
Kıymalı: minced meat and tomatoes
Sukuklu: spicy Turkish sausages
Yumurtlu: egg
Kusbasili: lamb in a spicy tomato sauce
Karasir: all of the above
Pul Biber: crushed chillis, sprinkled over the top

Anadolu Hisarı ★★★

This pretty village, guarded by an imposing but ruined fortress, is another great place to stop and soak up the atmosphere. The original **fortress** was built in the late 14th century by Sultan Beyazid I, on the site of a former temple to Zeus. For centuries it functioned as a lookout point and a guard to the narrowest point of the Bosphorus River and was reinforced by Mehmet the Conqueror before he invaded Constantinople. After the conquest of the city in 1453, the settlement outside the walls of the fortress began to grow, with army barracks, mosques, a hamam, houses and schools, as well as several imposing mansions along the Bosphorus.

Two narrow rivers, the Göksu and the Küçüksu, flow into the Bosphorus either side of Anadolu Hisarı and, in the 19th century, the meadows around these streams became very popular for **picnicking** upper class families at weekends, with people arriving in caiques and canoes laden with food and drink. The sultans and their entourages would come in their imperial barges and survey the scene. Today, everybody who lives here has a boat and pleasure craft are often moored two deep under the overhanging trees, although the grander mansions have been torn down and the meadows are now occupied by the **Marmara University Sports College**. Sadly, the water of the stream is rather polluted, too. But many of the houses on the Bosphorus are still in superb condition, despite their age, painted in bright colours with sunny wooden decks overlooking the water and lush gardens. As the fortress is ruined, there are no opening times and visitors can clamber over the walls to look inside.

Below: *Anadolu Hisarı is ruined, but was once an important lookout point over the Bosphorus.*

Küçüksu *

Just before the stream of the same name flows into the Bosphorus is the Küçüksu Kasrı (open 09:30–17:00, closed Mondays and Thursdays), a petite, two-storey marble **palace** constructed for Abdülmecit in 1856 by Nikogos Balyan, the son of the architect who built the Dolmabahçe Palace. This Baroque creation is white, and is lavishly furnished with ornate mirrors, chandeliers and superb Italian marble fireplaces. It was once used by Atatürk and it was turned into a museum in 1983.

Above: *The views are spectacular where the narrow Bosphorus meets the vast expanse of the Black Sea.*

Beylerbeyi Sarayı **

Just before the Bosphorus Bridge is the most dramatic **palace** on the Asian side of the Bosphorus, Beylerbeyi Sarayı (open 09:30–17:00, closed Mondays and Thursdays), an opulent waterfront creation in gleaming white marble. This magnificent palace was built in 1865 for Abdülaziz by Serkis Balyan. Abdülhamid II later lived here after being deposed, and after his death in 1819 the palace was used as a summer home in which to receive foreign dignitaries.

There are 26 rooms in the palace, all adorned with sumptuous carpets, chandeliers and vases. Guided tours are compulsory. Don't miss the beautiful palace **gardens**, shaded by magnolia trees, or the two smaller villas in the grounds, Sertab Mansion and Yellow Mansion.

From here, the ferry tours pass under the bridge and head back past the more industrialized area of the Asian shore. To explore the suburbs on this side, it is best to take a commuter ferry across from Eminönü or Beşiktaş; they run every 30 minutes and you can spend as long as you like wandering around.

NIGHT CRUISES

If you are travelling on a budget and cannot afford one of the dinner cruises that make their way up and down the **Bosphorus**, you can enjoy the same view simply by taking one of the **ferries** across to Asia and back. You can sit up on deck with a drink, admire the beautiful night skyline of the city and spot the bobbing lights of fishing boats and the sweeping beams of the big oil tankers. The journey across to Üsküdar or Kadıköy takes about 20 minutes in each direction, so for the price of a beer, you have a ready-made 40-minute cruise.

7
The Princes' Islands

Like the woods and villages along the Bosphorus, the **Princes' Islands** represent the green lungs of Istanbul and are a delightful retreat in summer when the heat and dust become too much. Located just off the coast in the **Sea of Marmara**, the nine islands, four of which can be visited, have the feeling of sleepy villages, their old wooden villas set under fragrant pines and narrow pathways leading through the woods to pebbly beaches.

The islands, located some 20km (12 miles) southeast of Istanbul, were formerly known as the **Panadanisia**, or Priests' Islands, for the monks and hermits who came here to meditate. The Byzantine name, Kızıl Adalar, or Princes' Islands, comes from the royals and nobles who were kept in **exile** here during the Byzantine era, a fate far easier than life in some of the mainland prisons.

Büyükada is the largest and most attractive of the islands, covered with pines and in spring, wild flowers. **Kınalıada**, the closest to Istanbul and the most arid, is known as the henna island because of its red-coloured cliffs. **Burgazada**, with its sheltered harbour, is lined with lavish summer homes and mansions, while **Heybeliada** has some smart hotels and is home to the Turkish Naval Academy.

Of the smaller islands, **Sedef** has a smattering of villas, while **Yassi** is occupied by part of Istanbul University. **Kaşik** is privately owned, while **Sivriada** and **Tavşanada** are uninhabited. Slow and high-speed ferries run from Eminönü to the four largest islands, although some wealthy locals moor their own boats here.

DON'T MISS

*** Büyükada:** one of the prettiest islands, with superb fish restaurants.
** **Monastery of St George:** ancient hilltop church on Büyükada.
** **Heybeliada:** famous for its ornate wooden mansions.
* **Sait Faik Museum, Burgazada:** visit the former home of Turkey's famous author.
* **Yörük Ali Plajları:** comprises two lovely beaches with basic facilities.

Opposite: *Beautiful Büyükada is an escape from the heat of the city.*

Above: *A horse-drawn carriage is the best way to get around the islands.*

Visit the islands for a day trip, or to really soak up the atmosphere, stay for a few nights, sampling the wonderful fish restaurants and exploring the beaches. Needless to say, the archipelago is packed in summer and it can be difficult to find accommodation. But spring, autumn and midweek days in the hottest months are quieter times.

The earliest records of human habitation on the islands are under Constantius, who built **monastaries** here as places of exile for enemies of the empire. In the conquest of Istanbul, all the islands except Büyükada surrendered, Büyükada lasting over 40 days until caving in, after which the monasteries were deserted. Greeks, Armenians and a handful of British built homes on the islands in the 19th century, when the journey from Istanbul by **caique** took three hours, and the advent of big passenger ferries led to the large-scale development of holiday homes.

Today, locals bemoan the fact that the islands have become over-commercialized. While most new buildings are still in sympathy with the traditional style, it is only a matter of time before somebody scars the landscape with a big, concrete hotel. The main saving grace of the

---

A DOG'S LIFE

The smallest of the Princes' Islands, the uninhabited **Kopek Adasi**, was once the home of hundreds of stray dogs, rounded up from the streets of Istanbul and dumped in the wilderness, where there was no running water, to fend for themselves. The dogs' howls echoing across the sea at night disturbed the residents of the neighbouring islands and the animals were later disposed of.

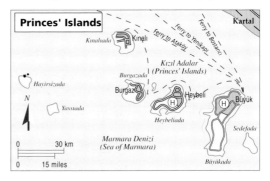

islands is the ban on domestic cars, which means that everyone gets around by bicycle or **horse-drawn carriage**. But the Sea of Marmara is horribly polluted compared to the crystal clear waters Istanbul's thirty-somethings can remember from their childhood, and anyone looking to buy a holiday home nowadays heads much further south along the Anatolian coast, where they can at least swim in the sea.

Kınalıada

Kınalıada	N

Kınalıada Camii●

Hristos Monastırı

0   5 km

0   3 miles   Marmara Denizi (Sea of Marmara)

Kınalıada

Kınalıada is the closest island in the archipelago to the mainland, just 15 minutes away by high-speed ferry. It is also the most barren of the islands, its red cliffs giving rise to the name '**henna island**'. Because of its proximity to the city and a relative lack of forest, Kınalıada gives the impression of being rather overdeveloped but is still worth a visit if you only have an afternoon.

During Byzantine times, this island constantly came under attack from pirates. There were originally three monasteries here, two of which were destroyed before the arrival of Mehmet the Conqueror. One, Hristos, is still standing. It was built by Romanos Diogenis IV, who was exiled here in 1071. During the 20th century the monastery had various uses: first as an orphanage for girls, then between 1914 and 1917 as a military base, and later it was used by the **Red Cross**.

The island itself was developed by the Armenians and Greeks, descendants of whom remain here today. There is not much to see, although there are some pleasant **seafood cafés** along the narrow strip of pebbled beach. Look out, too, for the futuristic **mosque**, built in 1964 and located on the shore. The dome is built of two glass-enclosed pyramids and the minaret is a sharply pointed triangle.

ISLANDS IN THE SUN

The Princes' Islands seem to enjoy a **microclimate** of their own and are often sunny when Istanbul is in cloud. With less pollution hanging over them than the mainland has to endure, the air is clearer here and the winter mists are less dense.

Nonetheless, there is very little going on out of season; holiday homes are shut down, hotels closed and restaurants mainly boarded up. This can be a good time to visit, if you like to escape the crowds and wander around in peace.

Below: *Kınalıada is built up quite densely in places with holiday residences.*

Burgazada   N

Sait Faik
Müzesi

Ioannes Prodromos
Kilisesi

0   5 km

0   3 miles

Marmara Denizi/Sea of Marmara

BURGAZADA

Burgazada is one of the prettiest and most peaceful islands, with mewing seagulls circling above the ferry dock and fishermen selling the day's catch at the quayside. The Greek name for the island, Panormos, means '**safe harbour**', and for centuries the only inhabitants here were Greek fishermen. In the 1950s a **Jewish** community grew up here, and today most of the residents are wealthy families from Istanbul.

The best way to get around Burgazada is in one of the horse-drawn carriages lined up at the dock. To reach most of the island's 'beaches' – in reality smooth, rocky outcrops – you have to hike down through the pine woods. The best place for swimming, if the pollution doesn't put you off, is the **Kalpazankaya Rocks**, but this area tends to become crowded in summer. Just inland, you will notice the domed Ioannes Prodromos church, a Greek Orthodox church built in 1896 on the site of another church built in 842.

Sait Faik Museum *

This tiny museum is dedicated to the Turkish novelist Sait Faik, famous for his short stories. Stroll through his immaculate white wooden villa and you will gain a vivid impression of his life on the island and how it inspired his stories of love, nature and the sea.

HEYBELIADA

Heybeliada is the second-largest of the Princes' Islands, cloaked in bottle green pines and famous for its ornate wooden mansions, many of them brilliant in summer with purple bougainvillea.

During the Byzantine era, this island was known as **Demonisos** and **Halki**, the names inspired by an amazingly rich copper mine here. The copper was of such a high quality that it was supposed to be able to restore sight, though the mine was only briefly exploited in the 19th century, closing down when it was no longer viable.

Further prestige was gained from the establishment of the **Naval Academy** here in 1834, on the seafront at Kalyoncu. Although the actual academy has now moved, the building still serves as the Naval High School. Another landmark is the Greek Orthodox School of Theology, perched in the hills on a site occupied by a Greek monastery since the 9th century. The building, which was built in 1896, is not, however, open to the public.

Above: *The lack of cars makes the Princes' Islands a haven of peace.*
Opposite: *Fishing is still a good source of revenue for the islanders.*

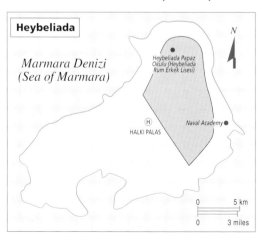

Heybeliada

Marmara Denizi (Sea of Marmara)

N

Heybeliada Papaz Okulu (Heybeliada Rum Erkek Lisesi)

Ⓗ HALKI PALAS

Naval Academy ●

| 0 | 5 km |
| 0 | 3 miles |

MEERSCHAUM

Meerschaum ('sea foam' in German) is a soft, white, clay-like, heat-resistant material generally made into pipes but jewellery and cigarette holders are also fashioned from it. Abroad it is an expensive commodity but is very cheap to buy in Istanbul. The largest and finest beds of meerschaum are found in **Eskişehir**, in Anatolia, the centre of the Turkish meerschaum industry.

Most people pass the time on Heybeliada by strolling on the marked trails and paved pathways through the pine forests, swimming, windsurfing and sailing, and enjoying the superb seafood restaurants around the jetty. For something a bit more upmarket, the **Halki Palas** hotel, nestling among the pine trees, is a grand old villa, recently modernized, with a fine restaurant.

Above: *Feta cheese is a salty, crumbly goat's cheese used mainly in salads.*

SAY 'CHEESE'

Turkey's best-known cheese is **feta**, a fragrant, crumbly, white goat's cheese, although if Greece has its way, a new EU law will mean that only cheese from Greece will be able to use the name. Look out for **lor** – a soft, creamy cheese like mascarpone – and **dil peyniri**, which tastes like mozzarella. Cheese is likely to appear sliced at the breakfast table or as part of a *meze* for dinner. Look out for feta preserved in flavoured olive oils, or cubed and sprinkled over a fresh farmer's salad consisting of cucumber, mint, tomato and olive.

BÜYÜKADA

The largest and, according to many, the most beautiful of the Princes' Islands, Büyükada is also the busiest. Its resident population of approximately 7000 swells to over 100,000 in summer, flocking here for the beaches, shops, restaurants, and the generally laid-back pace of life. The urban sprawl of the mainland is clearly visible, often shrouded in an ochre haze of **smog**, making this corner of paradise even more of a welcome escape.

Büyükada has been settled since Byzantine times, mainly by monks living in isolated monasteries in the hills. The first commercial ferry service started in 1846 and, between then and the early 20th century, exquisite wooden villas sprang up around the shores. Büyükada was considered a place of **political exile** until quite recently; **Trotsky** was banished here in the 1920s.

The island used to be inhabited by several Greek families and one of its most striking buildings, Rum Yetinhanesi, served as a Greek **orphanage** for many years, its bread and meat supplied by the Sultan. The building, a massive, foreboding, dark mansion perched high on the Isa Hill, is the largest free-standing wooden structure in the world today, although it is dangerously unstable and overrun by sheep and goats. Despite its historical and architectural interest, there are plans to tear it down to make way for a resort hotel, complete with a huge marina and a cable car down to the shore.

The best way to enjoy Büyükada is by horse-drawn carriage. The tour to the opposite end of the island and back takes about an hour and a half; ask for the *büyük tur*. The architecture is wonderfully quirky, right from the moment you arrive at the domed, Art Nouveau pier. Some of the wooden villas have been immaculately restored, painted in white and cream with colourful, louvred shutters and ornate carvings on the façades, while others are sadly peeling and crumbling away, their windows broken and their balconies worryingly slanted. Some of the most impressive houses are on the street **Kadiyoran Caddesi**, the smartest ones being the closest to the little town. Many have exquisite gardens, some ornate and formal and others a carefully cultivated tangle of honeysuckle, rose and colourful wild flowers sloping down to the water's edge.

Ask your carriage driver to show you the villa where Abdülhamid II's son lived; it is one of the most carefully preserved. Look out, too, for the **John Pasha Konak**, an elaborate mansion built in 1880 for John Pasha, the director of the steamer company which first linked the islands with the mainland. The building is typical in style of the grand mansions of the time. Just along the road from here is the Izzet Pasha mansion, built by a wealthy banker at the end of the 19th century. It was here that Leon Trotsky lived as a refugee from 1929 to 1933 and also wrote his autobiography.

> ### MUSIC IN TURKEY
>
> If you stumble across a folk festival, you are likely to see a few unfamiliar-looking musical instruments. Look out for the following:
> **Kemençe** – a three-stringed violin, played upright while balanced on the knees. The base string is plucked
> **Keman** – a different type of violin
> **Kanun** – a complex instrument with 72 strings, played with a plectrum
> **Saz** – a stringed instrument with a long neck – the frets, unlike those on a guitar, are moveable
> **Ney** – a reed flute with a horn mouthpiece

Below: *John Pasha's House was built for the director of the steamer company which served the mainland.*

Monastery of St George **

This monastery is located on the island's highest hill, a tiring, 203m (666ft) climb up through the pine trees. Legend has it that there was a monastery here in the 10th century and that the monks, on seeing the Crusaders advancing across the sea, hurriedly buried their precious **icon** of St George outside, marking the spot with an altar. A priest unearthed the icon in the 17th century and a new church was built. The structure here today is just 100 years old but, like many Greek Orthodox churches, it is exquisitely decorated. The interior is wonderfully calming, with its cool marble floors, gold stars painted on a blue ceiling arching away like the heavens, and a lovely white altar adorned with highly polished gold leaf.

Muslims and Christians alike make a **pilgrimage** here on St George's feast day, 24 April, tying scraps of cloth to the branches of the trees along the route up the hill as they pray for a cure. You can take a carriage or ride a donkey about halfway up the hill to an area called Lunapark, after which there is a cobblestoned pavement. There is a fairly basic restaurant at the top where you can sip chilled local wine and admire the view.

Hotel Splendid *

Do stop at the Hotel Splendid which, as its name implies, is a splendid, if faded, tribute to the better days it has seen. The hotel, with its dazzling white wooden façade and red shutters, was built in 1906 along the lines of the Hotel Negresco in Nice, although it is typically Turkish inside, with its rooms overlooking a central courtyard. The metallic domes on the roof hide giant cisterns, vital when there was no supply of fresh water on the islands and everything had to be brought by boat.

Left: *The coastline of Büyükada is full of lovely picnic spots.*
Opposite: *The Hotel Splendid is straight out of another age, its elegant rooms overlooking a peaceful courtyard.*

Kaymakamlik *

This beautiful three-storey mansion was once a private home, then it became a hotel, and nowadays it serves as administrative offices. The garden is part Oriental and part French, while the building itself has wonderful features, including intricate Rococo ceilings in its porches. During working hours, the security guards may let you get close enough for a photograph and a quick look.

Yörük Ali Plajları *

Where the island's little town meets the pine forest, at the end of Nizam Caddesi, a 500m (547yd) spit of land is fringed by two pretty beaches, part rock and part sand, complete with basic facilities. The area does get rather busy in summer but it is a good place to swim if you are not put off by the pollution in the Sea of Marmara.

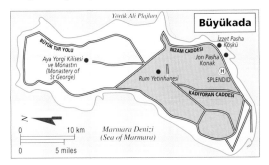

CHEERS!

You will come across a few strange-sounding drinks in Istanbul. **Rakı** is aniseed-flavoured grape brandy, not unlike the French *pastis*. **Sahlep** is a warming hot milk and tapioca root concoction, while **boza** is a thick drink made of millet and **ayran** is a yoghurt drink. If your tastes are more conservative, **Efes**, the local lager beer, is excellent, and **neskafe** is the generic term for instant coffee. If you want mineral water, ask for **maden suyu**, while tea is **çay**. Whisky, vodka and gin are easy to remember: **viski**, **votka** and **cin**. Be warned, though, that a request for a gin and tonic may be granted with a lot more gin than tonic.

8
Asian Istanbul and Beyond

Also known as '**Old Istanbul**', the Asian side of the city is quite a contrast to the European side. The pace of life is more relaxed, and at weekends the streets are packed with market stalls, people sitting in the sun playing backgammon and whole families out strolling.

The area is mainly residential and the ethnic mix is an easygoing melting pot of Armenians, Greeks, Jews and Turks. The two main settlements, **Üsküdar** and **Kadiköy**, which have now merged in the urban sprawl, started out as farming villages at the time of the conquest of Istanbul. By the 19th century both had become popular summer **resorts** characterized by grand mansions built by the **Ottomans**. It was only in the 20th century with the construction of the first Bosphorus Bridge that residential development on a large scale took off. Both suburbs are important dormitory towns for Istanbul's main business district across the water, and the greener areas around their outskirts are considered fashionable places to live.

There is plenty to enjoy on this side of the Bosphorus. From the water, admire the legendary **Leander's Tower**, Istanbul's most famous lighthouse. Üsküdar has several pretty **mosques**, and for the best views in Istanbul you should take a dolmuş up **Çamlıca Hill**, from where the whole skyline stretches out in front of you. Kadiköy has a wonderful pedestrian **shopping** zone and some fine restaurants, where the experience will be more genuinely Turkish than that on the European side. Further afield, there are some fascinating day trips to **Edirne**, **Bursa** and the battlefields of **Gallipoli**.

DON'T MISS

** **Çamlıca Hill:** the best views of Istanbul's skyline and the Bosphorus.
** **Üsküdar:** visit the pretty town square, surrounded by exquisite mosques.
** **Kadiköy:** lovely old town with superb food shopping and atmospheric cafés.
** **Gallipoli:** tour poignant battlefields and cemeteries.
* **Edirne:** regional town with markets and mosques.
* **Bursa:** visit the spectacular tomb of Mehmet I.
* **Leander's Tower:** Istanbul's most famous lighthouse, steeped in legend.

Opposite: *Some houses on the Asian shore date back to the Ottoman era.*

LEANDER'S TOWER

The legend of **Leander** and **Hero**, although belonging in the Dardanelles, a couple of hundred miles to the south, has long been attached to Leander's Tower. According to the Roman poet **Ovid**, Leander was in love with Hero, a priestess of Aphrodite, and swam to be with her in her tower every night. One night, a storm extinguished the light of the lighthouse and Leander drowned. Heartbroken, Hero commited suicide when she found his corpse the next day.

ENVIRONS OF ÜSKÜDAR
Leander's Tower *

This famous lighthouse, which guards the straits just outside Üsküdar, in fact has nothing to do with the legend of Leander. But as it has been here in one form or another since the 13th century, it is a fixture in the eyes of any local and appears in countless paintings, maps and photographs over the centuries.

The original building is believed to have been built by the Byzantine emperor Manuel Comnenos in the 13th century to defend the Bosphorus. Mehmet the Conqueror replaced the castle-like structure with his own tower when he conquered the city in 1453. In 1510, a huge earthquake damaged the tower, later repaired by Sultan Selim I Yavuz, who fitted it with oil lamps and created a lighthouse. The tower was a handy **prison**, too, and various political prisoners were incarcerated here.

In 1719, strong winds blew the oil lamps over and the tower burnt down. It was rebuilt in its current form by Ibrahim Paşa and was used as a **quarantine hospital** in the great 1830 cholera epidemic. It has been used as a lighthouse ever since, its red and white lights flashing every three seconds through the night. It has also been leased out to a company which plans to transform it into a restaurant. For now, however, visitors have to admire it from the water: there are great views from both the Üsküdar and Kadıköy ferries.

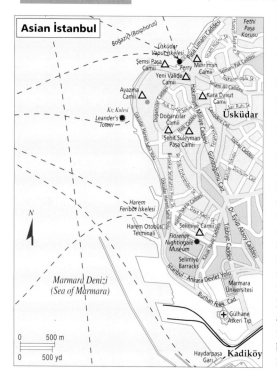

Asian İstanbul

Üsküdar *

Üsküdar is just a short hop from the European side by ferry and is well worth a visit for its street markets, mosques and views of the European side. If you are driving, you have to take the longer route across the Bosphorus Bridge, so do avoid the rush hour.

This area has been settled since around 500BC, when there was a village at Chalcedon, near what is today Kadiköy. It was here that **Byzas** arrived with a message from the Oracle at Delphi to found a colony 'opposite the blind', which he duly did, on the strategically important opposite shore of the Bosphorus.

There are a number of noteworthy mosques around Üsküdar's main, tree-lined square, Hakimiyeti Milliye Meydanı. On the northeast side is the **Dock Mosque**, or more romantically, Mihrimah Sultan Camii, built in 1548 for Sultan Süleyman's daughter, Mihrimah. Sinan, the architect of this mosque, also designed the Şemsi Paşa Camii in 1580, located to the west of the square, overlooking the sea. South of the square is the grand Yeni Valide Camii, or **Queen Mother's Mosque**, built by Sultan Ahmet III in 1710 for his mother, who is buried here.

The most interesting mosque is the unprepossessing Çinili Camii, or **Tiled Mosque**, in the suburb of Tabaklar, half an hour's walk or a quick taxi ride uphill. Built in the 17th century for Valide Sultan Kösem, the mosque's interior is brilliant with astonishing Iznik tiles.

Beşiktaş
Bosphorus
Ümraniye
Leander's • Üsküdar
Tower
Eminönü
Çamlıca
Kadiköy
• Florence Nightingale
Museum
Marmara Denizi
(Sea of Marmara)
Erenköy

THE ART OF RAKI DRINKING

Rakı is 45 per cent proof and is not to be taken lightly. It can induce a special high, a deep discussion, extreme emotions and a rather spectacular hangover.

There are three ways to drink rakı. The quickest way to oblivion is **neat**, down in one. The traditional way is to add a little **water** and some ice, making it turn cloudy. A third method, almost as potent as the first, is to take a sip of rakı, hold it in your mouth and sip a little water, **mixing** it in your mouth before swallowing.

Rakı is best accompanied by food and goes perfectly with *meze*. Not only does this complement the flavour but it lessens the after-effects.

Left: *Plenty of wealthy Turks live on the Asian side and commute to the city.*

DANCES

Turkey has several dances specific to certain regions.
Spoon Dance: from Konya. The rhythm of the dance is tapped out by the dancers on wooden spoons.
Sword and Shield Dance: from Bursa. Men create the music by clashing swords against shields, while dancing to celebrate the Ottoman conquest of the city.
The Karsilama: from Eastern Turkey. Lines of girls and boys face each other, singing alternately as they dance.
Horon Dance: from the Black Sea region. An energetic dance by men in black.

Florence Nightingale Museum *

At Üsküdar's Selimiye Barracks, there is a small museum (open 09:00–17:00, Saturdays only) dedicated to the work of Florence Nightingale, who worked here in awful conditions during the Crimean War (1853–56), establishing what is regarded as the basics of modern nursing practice.

Çamlıca **

This suburb sprawls across Istanbul's two highest hills, the peak rising to 261m (856ft) above sea level. A huge television transmission tower marks the top of the hill, but don't let that put you off. The views are breathtaking, as far as the **Princes' Islands** in one direction, out across the **Old City** to the west and to the north, and along the **Bosphorus**, glinting blue in the sun as it twists its way between Europe and Asia.

In the 18th century, this was a fashionable area in which to live, with grand wooden mansions and summerhouses springing up on the cool, wooded hills. Vineyards stretched from here down to Üsküdar on the shore, giving the area the name Baglarbası, or **Vineyard Peak**.

In the 1960s and 1970s, the area became overrun with illegal housing and fell into decline. In 1980, however, the hilltop was landscaped and turned into a park, which is understandably popular at weekends. The park is somewhat scruffier now but there are tea gardens from which to admire the view.

Below: *There is more green space on Istanbul's Asian side than in the European area.*

Üsküdar   Çamlıca

Kadıköy

Florence Nightingale
Museum   Haydarpaşa Garı

*Marmara Denizi
(Sea of Marmara)*

Left: *Kadiköy has a lively,
colourful market and,
because there are no cars,
it is a wonderful place to
explore on foot.*

KADIKÖY

The streets of Kadıköy are a wonderful experience, alive
with market traders, fresh fish and vegetable stalls and
the aroma of freshly baked bread wafting out from the
numerous bakeries and patisseries. The town centre,
around five minutes' walk from the ferry terminal, has
been declared a conservation area and there are no cars,
so it is pleasant to walk around the old cobbled streets.

At the time of the conquest of Istanbul in 1453,
Kadıköy was little more than a Greek fishing village,
surrounded by vineyards and orchards. Turkish inhabitants did not arrive until the early 18th century, when a
mosque was built here, followed by Armenians and
later, Jews. The **Ottomans** favoured the town as a country
resort but by the end of the 19th century, the area was
built up and less fashionable as a weekend retreat.

The main street to explore is Muvakkithane Caddesi,
which takes its name from the proliferation of **clock**
and watch shops that was once here. Look out for a confectioner's shop called **Haci Bekir**, its windows lined
with old-fashioned candy jars full of colourful boiled
sweets, great piles of Turkish Delight, sugared almonds,
macaroons and sticky halva. The shop has been here for
80 years. Opposite, the Albanian-run patisserie Baylan
has been in existence for 40 years.

JUST DESSERTS

Whoever heard of chicken
for dessert? Well, if you
come across **tavuk göğsü**
on a menu, it is your big
chance to try it. Chicken
breast is thinly shredded and
cooked with milk, sugar,
vanilla and a kind of gum.
When the whole concoction
is cool and solid, it is cut into
squares, rolled into sausages
and sprinkled with cinnamon
before being served cold.

Another version of this
delicacy, **Kazandibi**, is
prepared in the same way
but slightly burned. If you
want the flavours but not
the chicken, **sitlac**, or rice
pudding, is a more palatable
version, made with rice
instead of fowl.

Above: *Bread in the form of giant pretzels from a street vendor is a popular snack in Istanbul.*
Opposite: *The Selimiye Mosque is one of the city's most beautiful.*

GET STUFFED

The shared taxi or **dolmuş**, which means 'stuffed' in Turkish, is a national institution and a cheap, practical way of getting around. In Istanbul the dolmuş is often a classic American gas guzzler, such as a 1950s Chevrolet or Cadillac, but these are being superseded by less romantic but practical minibuses. The dolmuş operates over a fixed route but can be flagged down anywhere on the way, and its destination is generally written on a windscreen placard. On a busy urban route it is better to take the dolmuş from the start of its run at a stand marked by a 'D' sign.

Also on this street is the small Armenian **church** of Surp Takavor, built in 1858. On nearby Yasa Caddesi is the Greek Orthodox church of the Christian martyr Saint Euphemia, with beautiful frescoes and an elaborate, gilded altar. Close to the church is an even older institution than Haci Bekir and Baylan; the Beyaz Firin **bakery** has been on this site for 150 years and is famous for its breads, pastries and puddings.

The area around Kadiköy's ferry terminal is another place for local colour, particularly at weekends. All along the seafront (with, admittedly, not especially enchanting views of the docks) are cafés and bars where people sit outside on wooden benches drinking tea. Inland from here on Sundays is a rather incongruous **pet market**, housed in tin huts that fold out to reveal a whole alley of bird cages, cat and dog accessories and even tropical fish.

Also worth looking out for, if only as the ferry comes in to dock, is the **Haydarpaşa Gari**, the main railway station serving Istanbul on the Asian side, bringing some 110,000 passengers to the city every day. The station was a gift from the German emperor Willem II following his visit to Istanbul in 1898. Designed by architects Otto Ritter and Helmut Cuno, it was completed in 1908 and has recently been restored. The European architecture looks grand and imposing but somewhat out of place in the context of Asian Istanbul.

EDIRNE

Some 230km (143 miles) west of Istanbul, across rolling plains towards the Greek border, is the town of Edirne. The town was founded in AD125 by Hadrian and was called Hadrianopolis, and later Adrianople, until the Turks renamed it in the 14th century.

Edirne was actually the Ottoman capital from 1362, although Sultan Murat I moved his centre of power to Constantinople in 1458. Today, it is rather a sleepy, agricultural town, its main attraction being a number of beautiful mosques.

Selimiye Camii **

This is one of the most beautiful mosques imaginable, constructed by Mimar Sinan, the architect responsible for the **Süleyman Mosque** in Istanbul. Its four minarets are surpassed in height only by those on the mosque in Mecca and the amazing dome is similar in size to that of Aya Sofya in Istanbul. Sunlight streams in through hundreds of windows; according to local legend, Sultan Selim II, for whom the mosque was built, considered 999 windows to be a lucky number.

Grand Bazaar *

Near the 12th-century Clock Tower, the only remaining part of the Roman walls, this barrel-vaulted bazaar, exuding a variety of exotic sights, sounds and smells, is one of the oldest in Turkey.

GREASE WRESTLING

The **Kırkpınar Wrestling Championships** take place every summer, depending on Ramazan, at Edirne, attracting contestants and spectators from all over the country. The rules are few; the participants cover themselves in olive oil and wear special leather shorts. The loser is the first to be pinned to the ground, or to collapse. Winning can mean incredible prestige for a town or village.

Below: *The Green Mosque is constructed from very expensive marble.*

BURSA

Another longish day trip by boat, bus or road, or a short flight, Bursa is 240km (149 miles) south of Istanbul, at the southeast corner of the Sea of Marmara. The town sprawls over the foothills of **Mount Olympus of Mysia**, or Uludag in Turkish, and is surrounded by yew and cypress trees. In 1326, Bursa was capital of the Ottoman Empire, a somewhat short-lived honour as the capital soon moved to Edirne. The town proceeded to develop a silk-weaving industry and, while traces of this remain, it is known today for car manufacturing. Visitors come to Bursa for its fabulous Islamic art collections. If you plan to visit Iznik as well, it is a good idea to stay the night.

Yeşil Türbe and Yeşil Camii **

Sultan Mehmet I built this beautiful mosque, the Green Mosque, in 1424 and was so impressed with its luxurious marble and exquisite tiles that he actually lived in it. Just opposite is the Green Mausoleum, where he is buried, a domed, octagonal building covered with dazzling turquoise tiles. Mehmet's sarcophagus is inside, as are those of members of his family.

Museum of Turkish and Islamic Art *

Housed in the theological school, part of the mosque complex, this museum (open 08:00–12:00 and 13:00–17:00 Tuesday–Sunday, 10:00–13:00 Monday) is best known for its puppet collection. Made of cardboard and camel leather, the comical puppets of **Karagöz and Hacivat**, based on real characters, have been used in travelling shows for centuries. They are the Turkish equivalent of the British Punch and Judy puppet shows.

GALLIPOLI

Anyone with an interest in modern military history will want to make the pilgrimage to the tragic battlefields of Gallipoli, now a national park in the southwest corner of the Sea of Marmara. Aim to make this a two-day trip, spending the night in Çanakkale, and pay a visit to the ancient city of Troy nearby at the same time.

Gallipoli is the place where Winston Churchill ordered the **Allied forces** in World War I to invade the Gallipoli peninsula and take the **Dardanelles**, a narrow strait leading into the Sea of Marmara. The troops, consisting of Australian, New Zealand, British and French soldiers, invaded on 25 April 1915 and managed to last for eight months in terrible conditions, during which time 250,000 lives were lost and no progress made. The Turkish forces suffered just as badly.

On a guided tour, you can visit the narrow trenches, which are still visible, as well as the beaches, the information centre at Kabatepe, with its relics and mementoes of this terrible time, and the most poignant sight of all, row after row of small, carefully tended gravestones. Gallipoli is a sad place, its calm and beauty today far removed from the atrocities that happened here. Australia and New Zealand, both of which sustained huge losses here, still commemorate 25 April as **Anzak Day** in honour of those who died.

Above: *The cemetery at Gallipoli is a moving and poignant sight.*
Overleaf: *The Grand Bazaar is an Aladdin's Cave of bargains.*

IZNIK

By the time you have visited so many mosques and admired so many Iznik tiles, you will be curious to see where this beautiful art originated. Iznik is located 80km (50 miles) northeast of Bursa on the shores of the Iznik lake and is still surrounded by old walls.

All that is left of the tile production, at its height in the 14th century, is the small **Iznik Museum** which contains several **original tiles**. Tile production declined in the 16th century after a massive earthquake disrupted the work of the craftsmen in the many workshops but there are enough examples of their intricate work in mosques and monuments all over Turkey to have turned this small town into a legend.

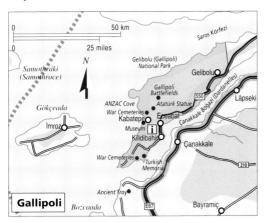

Istanbul at a Glance

Istanbul is at its most pleasant in **spring** and **autumn**, with warm sun and cooling sea breezes by day and balmy nights when a light jacket will suffice. **Summer** is fine if you don't mind tramping round the ancient sites in oppressive heat; during July and August, Bosphorus cruises and the beaches of the Princes' Islands beckon. December to February is to be avoided; it is generally chilly, wet and misty. Snow is not unknown.

Be aware that during the holy month of Ramazan (also known as Ramadan), it is impolite to eat, drink and smoke on the streets by day and you may have problems finding lunch. The festive atmosphere after sunset, however, means that this can be a good time to visit. The dates move every year, so check first with the Turkish Tourist Board.

GETTING THERE

Istanbul's Atatürk Airport is the main point of entry for visitors to Turkey. **Flights** operate from here to all over the world and the airport is one of the two home bases of Turkish Airlines which, through its Qualiflyer alliance with other European carriers, has a network that extends world-wide. Istanbul Airlines also operates out of Istanbul, serving main European cities.

Atatürk Airport, tel: (0212) 663-6400; **Turkish Airlines**, tel: (0212) 663-6363; **Istanbul Airlines**, tel: (0212) 231-7526.

A new terminal is presently under construction but, for the time being, Atatürk Airport is somewhat chaotic and crowded. Getting to baggage reclaim on arrival may take up to an hour. The journey downtown takes anything from 30 to 90 minutes, depending on the traffic. Buses go every 30 minutes from the arrivals area to Taksim Square and cost approximately a tenth of the price of a taxi.

Other points of entry into Turkey include the capital Ankara, as well as the charter destinations of Izmir and Dalaman, served during summer by numerous charter airlines from the main European cities.

Trains run from European cities, with direct services from Munich and Vienna taking around 35 hours. All trains come into Sirkeci station next to Eminönü, tel: (0212) 527-0051. Trains from Asia and the Middle East arrive at Haydarpaşa on the Asian side, tel: (0216) 336-0475.

It is also possible to enter Turkey by **road** from either Bulgaria or Greece, provided that the same driver takes the car out of the country within the permitted three-month stay. The main route for travel by road is via the E80 motorway through Bulgaria.

Ferries operate from Chios, Samos and Rodos in Greece to Turkish ports.

GETTING AROUND

Car rental is rather expensive and you are strongly advised to use public transport within the city, as the traffic is pretty awful and parking difficult. For trips outside the city, however, cars can be rented either for weekly, daily or weekend periods.
Avis: tel: (0212) 663-0646 or (0212) 241-2917 (at the Hilton Hotel);
Sun Rent A Car: tel: (0216) 318-9040.

Boats go to and fro across the Bosphorus between the European and Asian sides. The main departure points are Eminönü, Karaköy and Beşiktaş, sailing to Üsküdar and Kadiköy on the Asian side. Ferries depart every 15 or 30 minutes, depending on the destination, and the journey takes about 15 minutes to Üsküdar and 25 minutes to Kadiköy.

Cruises along the Bosphorus leave every day from the Eminönü jetty at 10:30, 12:45 and 14:10 (not on Sundays), allowing time for a lunch break at the mouth of the Black Sea before turning round; tel: (0212) 522-0045.

Istanbul at a Glance

The quickest way to get to the Princes' Islands is by catching the **fast sea bus**, which leaves from Kabatas on the European side. The journey takes anything from 20 minutes to one hour, depending on which island you are visiting; tel: (0216) 362-0444.

Buses are cheap but slow. The main terminus on the European side is Taksim Square, as well as Beşiktaş and Aksaray. On the Asian side, the bus stations are at Üsküdar, Kadiköy and Bostanci. Buy a ticket at a special kiosk before boarding the bus. You will have to learn to read some Turkish words to use the bus service as it is rare to find an English-speaking driver.

A **dolmuş** is a shared minibus with fixed fares. Each person pays according to the distance they travel. There are dolmuş stations at Taksim Square and Aksaray and the dolmuş will wait here until they are full. It is more expensive than a bus but cheaper than a taxi and nearly as comfortable.

Yellow **taxis** are plentiful and thanks to the strength of the dollar and the pound, reasonably cheap for visitors. All taxis are metered and can easily be hailed on the street. Watch the number of zeros very carefully; while most taxi drivers are honest, it is quite a popular scam to allow a

flustered passenger to hand over a note ten times larger than the meter demands. It is customary to round up the fare as a tip. Be warned that almost all taxi drivers in Istanbul chain smoke!

Istanbul has assorted **tram** and **metro** lines, none of them of great relevance to visitors apart from the Tünel, with just two stops from Tünel to Karaköy, the oldest tramway in Europe. Trains run every ten minutes or so and the journey is more for novelty than a serious form of transport. A more modern metro line runs westwards from Aksaray, eventually joining up with the suburban train line beyond the airport, while a second line runs eastwards from Aksaray to Sultanahmet. A new line runs from Taksim to the suburb of Levent, but this is aimed mainly at commuters.

WHERE TO STAY

Istanbul has abundant accommodation, although it is skewed mainly towards the middle and upper end of the price bracket. There are a number of hostels and backpacker hotels around Sultanahmet, but by far the most popular type of accommodation are the reasonably priced two- and three-star hotels, some modern, some in beautiful old restored buildings. Again, the vast majority of these hotels are

in Sultanahmet. Most rooms in these establishments will have their own private bathroom and a telephone. The smarter ones are air-conditioned and many have a breakfast room or small restaurant. For a slightly higher price, look for the 'boutique' hotels, most of which are located in buildings of historic interest. Most of them are featured in the brochure 'Charming Hotels of Turkey', available from the tourist board.

Almost all the business hotels in Istanbul are located in the modern part of the city, around Taksim Square, where there are several four- and five-star establishments, and in 'Conference Valley', a few minutes' walk further north. Most of the big names like Hyatt, Inter-Continental and Hilton are represented here, as well as several more, and there are also some very good, Turkish-owned four-star hotels. There is surprisingly little accommodation to be found along the Bosphorus and if you do opt to stay in this area, bear in mind that it will be a longish taxi journey to virtually any of the main sights. Similarly, there is very little on the Asian side of the Bosphorus; most visitors tend to keep this part of the city as a day trip. If you want to stay in one of the hotels on the Princes' Islands in summer, it is essential to book well in advance, as many of the locals rebook the same spot year after year and accommodation is therefore quite scarce.

A new business district has sprung up around the airport during the last decade or so and if you are catching an early flight and want to avoid the inevitable traffic jams on your way out of the city, it is worth considering spending your last night here.

Topkapı and Sultanahmet
LUXURY
Arena Hotel, Küçükayasofia Mah. Sehit, Mehmet Paşa Yokusu Üçler, Hamam Sokak 13–15, tel: (0212) 458-0364, fax: (0212) 458-0366. Most of the rooms in this attractive small hotel have views of the sea. The hotel has its own restaurant, hamam and airport shuttle.

Four Seasons Hotel, Tevkifhane Sokak 1, Sultanahmet, tel: (0212) 638-8200, fax: (0212) 638-8210. Housed in a neo-Classical building, this elegant hotel has five-star facilities as well as excellent views of both the Aya Sofya and the Blue Mosque.

Ayasofya Pensions, Sultanahmet, tel: (0212) 513-3660, fax: (0212) 513-3669. Accommodation here consists of a whole street of charming, painted wooden houses furnished with period pieces.

Yesil Ev, Kabasakal Caddesi 5, Sultanahmet, tel: (0212) 517-6785, fax: (0212) 517-6780. This is a charming old house with period décor, a lovely garden and an excellent restaurant.

MID-RANGE
Yusufpaşa, Cankurtaran Caddesi 40, Sultanahmet, tel: (0212) 458-0001, fax: (0212) 458-0009. A 19th-century mansion with 20 rooms and a pretty roof terrace overlooking the sea.

Çelal Sultan Hotel, Yerebatan Caddesi, Salkimsögüt Sokak 16, Sultanahmet, tel: (0212) 520-9323, fax: (0212) 522-9724. This renovated town house is just five minutes' walk from Topkapı Palace. It has 20 comfortable rooms.

Citadel Hotel, Ahirkapı Caddesi 9, Sultanahmet, tel: (0212) 516-2313, fax: (0212) 516-1384. Restored Ottoman mansion near old city walls, on the beach, a short walk from Topkapı Palace.

Hotel Fehmi Bay, Üçler Sokak 15, Sultanahmet, tel: (0212) 638-9083, fax: (0212) 518-1264. Small, attractive hotel on Hippodrome Square.

Hotel Sidera, Kadirga Meydani Dönüs Sokak 14, Kumkapı, tel: (0212) 638-3460, fax: (0212) 518-7262. A restored wooden house in fishing district of Kumkapı, just 10 minutes' walk from Topkapı Palace.

BUDGET
Green Hotel, Akbiyik Caddesi 5, Sultanahmet, tel: (0212) 458-1957, fax: (0212) 638-6600. This small, modern hotel with roof terrace is situated just outside Topkapı Palace.

Orient Youth Hostel, Akbiyik Caddesi 13, Sultanahmet, tel: (0212) 517-9493, fax: (0212) 518-3994. Dormitories as well as double rooms are available in this friendly youth hostel.

Hotel Nomade, Divan Yolu, Ticarethane Sokak 15, tel: (0212) 511-1236, fax: (0212) 513-2404. This hostel consists of double rooms, each with a private shower.

Guesthouse Berk, Kutlugün Sokak 27, Cankurtaran, tel: (0212) 516-9671, fax: (0212) 517-7715. This is a small, family-run guesthouse. The rooms each have their own private bathroom.

Hippodrom Pansiyon, Üçler Sokak 9, tel: (0212) 516-0902, no fax. This rather simple but squeaky clean pension is situated close to the Hippodrome.

Western Districts
LUXURY
Akgün, Adan Menderes Bulvarı, Topkapı, tel: (0212) 534-4879, fax: (0212) 534-9126. This is a large, modern five-star hotel, close to the old city gates (not Topkapı Palace).

Istanbul at a Glance

Eresin Topkapı, Millet Caddesi 186, Topkapı, tel: (0212) 631-1212, fax: (0212) 631-3702. A large business hotel with its own swimming pool, situated in the Topkapı business district.

Hotel Yigitalp, Laleli Gençtürk Caddesi, Çukur Çesme Sokak 38, tel: (0212) 512-9860, fax: (0212) 512-2072. This attractive four-star hotel with its original features is located in the Laleli district, near Aksaray.

MID-RANGE
Kariye Hotel, Kariye Camii Sokak 18, Edirnekapı, tel: (0212) 534-8414, fax: (0212) 521-6631. This restored Ottoman mansion has an excellent, traditional restaurant, and is situated next door to Chora Church.

Sunlight Hotel, Piyerloti Caddesi 60, Çemberlitas, tel: (0212) 638-9955, fax: (0212) 638-9960. This is a small, modern hotel in the very heart of 'Old Istanbul'. It boasts a rather attractive roof terrace.

Along the Bosphorus
LUXURY
Çırağan Palace Hotel Kempinski, Çırağan Caddesi, Beşiktaş, tel: (0212) 258-3377, fax: (0212) 259-6686. This is Istanbul's most luxurious hotel, partly built in an Ottoman palace, and situated in beautiful grounds on the Bosphorus.

Conrad International Istanbul, Barbaros Bulvarı, Beşiktaş, tel: (0212) 227-3000, fax: (0212) 259-6667. Large, modern, hilltop five-star with plenty of facilities as well as wonderful views of the Bosphorus.

Swissôtel The Bosphorus, Maçka, tel: (0212) 259-0101, fax: (0212) 259-0105. A superb business hotel with lots of resort facilities and extensive grounds overlooking the Bosphorus.

Ortaköy Princess, Dereboyu Caddesi 26/28, Ortaköy, tel: (0212) 227-6010, fax: (0212) 260-2148. This small five-star in the pretty village of Ortaköy has several restaurants and its own fitness centre.

MID-RANGE
Büyük Tarabya Hotel, Tarabya, tel: (0212) 262-1000, fax: (0212) 262-2260. A Turkish-owned hotel in the fishing village of Tarabya, towards the Black Sea.

Modern Istanbul
LUXURY
Hilton, Harbiye, tel: (0212) 231-4650, fax: (0212) 240-4165. A recently renovated five-star in 'Conference Valley' with good business and convention facilities.

Hyatt Regency, Taskisla Caddesi, Taksim, tel: (0212) 225-7000, fax: (0212) 225-7007. Luxurious five-star with excellent bars and restaurants near Taksim Square.

Ceylan Inter-Continental, Taksim, tel: (0212) 231-2121, fax: (0212) 231-2180. Luxury five-star on Taksim Square with good business facilities and international atmosphere.

The Marmara Istanbul, Taksim Square 80090, tel: (0212) 251-4696, fax: (0212) 244-0509. This is a tower block on Taksim Square with fantastic views and all the modern facilities.

Galata Residence Aparthotel, Bankalar Caddesi, Haci Ali Sokak 27, Galata, tel: (0212) 292-4841, fax: (0212) 244-2323. These two-bedroom apartments, with cooking facilities as well as a restaurant, are ideal for longer stays.

MID-RANGE
Hotel Divan, Elmadag, Taksim, tel: (0212) 231-4100, fax: (0212) 248-8527. This Turkish-owned four-star hotel is on Taksim Square. Its restaurant is quite famous and it has a friendly pub.

Vardar Palace Hotel, Siraselviler Caddesi 54, 80060 Taksim, tel: (0212) 252-2888, fax: (0212) 252-1527. This Ottoman-era hotel, with modern facilities, has 40 rooms.

Hotel Pera Palas, Mesrutiyet Caddesi 98, Tepebasi 80050, tel: (0212) 251-4560, fax: (0212) 251-4089. This hotel is a local legend, with its many original facilities, famous bar and restaurant.

Istanbul at a Glance

BUDGET
Otel Avrupa, Topçu Caddesi 32, Telimhane, tel: (0212) 250-9420, no fax. Good value singles and doubles in old apartment house.

Asian Istanbul
MID-RANGE
Harem Hotel, Ambar Sokak 2, Selimiye 81170, tel: (0216) 310-6800, fax: (0216) 334-7730. Attractive, 100-room three-star hotel with its own swimming pool.

Princes' Islands
LUXURY
Büyükada Princess, Iskele Caddesi 2, Büyükada, tel: (0216) 382-1628, fax: (0216) 382-1949. A luxurious, 24-room hotel housed in a 19th-century mansion.

MID-RANGE
Halki Palas, Heybeliada, tel: (0216) 351-9550, fax: (0216) 382-1949. Historic hotel with wonderful views on Heybeliada island.
Saydem Planet Hotel, Iskele Caddesi 1, Büyükada, tel: (0216) 382-2670, fax: (0216) 382-3848. This is the popular weekend haunt of Istanbul residents visiting Büyükada Island.
Splendid Palas, Birtat Restaurant, Gullistan Caddesi 10, Büyükada, tel: (0212) 382-1245. This is yet another beautifully restored mansion with an excellent restaurant.

Near the Airport
LUXURY
Crowne Plaza, Sahil Yolu, Ataköy, tel: (0212) 560-8100, fax: (0212) 560-8157. Modern business hotel overlooking the Sea of Marmara, 8km (5 miles) from the airport.

MID-RANGE
Çinar Hotel, Sevketiye Mah. Fener Mevkii, Yesilköy, tel: (0212) 663-2900, fax: (0212) 663-2921. Quiet business hotel in residential area near the airport.

WHERE TO EAT

Bear in mind that even luxury in Istanbul is affordable to most visitors, thanks to the weakness of the lira. Lunch is served from about noon, while most people eat dinner between 20:00 and 22:30, later in summer. Go easy on your meze order if you want to fit in a main course and the excellent Turkish desserts. Remember a salad is often served with the meze or before the main course. Try to stick to Turkish wines with your meal – not only do they complement the food better but they are also very reasonably priced.

Restaurants generally tend to be more expensive in Sultanahmet because of the tourist trade, but if you choose carefully you can find good food and some wonderful views of the famous sights. For a fast food lunch in an

action-packed day of sightseeing around the Hippodrome, there are several cafeteria-style restaurants along Divan Yolu.

In summer, don't miss the experience of dining outdoors with a view of the Bosphorus. It is very romantic and the seafood in the waterfront restaurants is excellent.

As a big, international city, Istanbul has a huge variety of restaurants, from pizza outlets to burger bars, as well as a smattering of Chinese, Indian, American, Russian and German. Most of the establishments listed below, however, feature authentic Turkish food served in attractive surroundings.

Sultanahmet
LUXURY
Rami, Utangaç Sokak 6, tel: (0212) 517-6593. Beautiful rooftop terrace with views of the Blue Mosque, serving Ottoman specialities. Book in advance.
Sarniç, Sogukçesme Caddesi, tel: (0212) 512-4291. Unusual Turkish menu in unusual setting – an old Roman cistern. Open Wednesday–Sunday.

MID-RANGE
Yesil Ev, Kabasakal Kaddesi 5, 34400 Sultanahmet, tel: (0212) 517-6786. Garden dining in restored 19th-century wooden mansion. Great meze, kebabs and decadent dessert trolley.

Istanbul at a Glance

Konyalı, Topkapı Palace, tel: (0212) 513-9696. Good but simple Turkish food in the grounds of Topkapı Palace. Lunch only. Closed Tuesdays.
Turkistan Asevi, Tavukhane Sokak. This restaurant serves Central Asian cuisine; cheese and mince-stuffed savoury pancakes are a speciality.

BUDGET
Lale Restaurant Pudding Shop, Sultanahmet Divan Yolu 6, tel: (0212) 522-2970. This restaurant is a famous former hippie haunt opposite Blue Mosque. Mezes, meatballs and kebabs.
Sultanahmet Köftecisi, Divan Yolu 12. Kebabs and meatballs at bargain prices.
Sultan Pub, Divan Yolu 2, tel: (0212) 526-6347. This pub is a popular meeting place serving sandwiches, drinks and Turkish apple tea.

Western Districts
MID-RANGE
Daruzziyafe, Sifahane Caddesi 6, 34430 Suleymaniye, tel: (0212) 511-8414. This atmospheric, 400-year-old restaurant is housed in the Suleyman Mosque. Delicious Ottoman specialities and freshly squeezed fruit juice.
Havuzlu Lokantasi, Gani Çelebi Sokak 3, Kapalı Çarşı, tel: (0212) 527-3346. An atmospheric restaurant in the covered market, serving Turkish specialities.

Orient House, Tiyatro Caddesi 27, Beyazit, tel: (0212) 517-3488. This restaurant serves excellent Turkish food and also offers belly dancing. It is, however, somewhat touristy.

BUDGET
Sevim Lokantasi, Koltuk Kazazlar, Kapalı Çarşı. Here visitors can eat kebab sandwiches and stews alongside the market traders.
Minas, Samsa Sokak 7, Kumkapı, tel: (0212) 522-9646. Seafood specialities are on offer in the busy fishing harbour. Be sure to ask for swordfish kebabs.

Modern Istanbul
LUXURY
Panorama Restaurant, The Marmara Hotel, Taksim Square 80090, tel: (0212) 251-4696. There are stunning views from this restaurant on the 20th floor. Meze, Turkish specialities and huge dessert selection available.
Park Samdam, Mim Kemal Öke Caddesi 18/1, tel: (0212) 225-0710. This restaurant offers French-Turkish cuisine and is very popular for business lunches. No credit cards are accepted.
Sark Sofrasi, Swissôtel The Bosphorus, tel: (0212) 259-0101. This traditional-style Turkish chalet serves a delicious selection of gourmet Ottoman food, beautifully cooked and presented.

MID-RANGE
Divan Hotel (see Where to Stay). A wonderful Turkish breakfast is served here, even to non-residents. The hotel also has a renowned restaurant and patisserie, both reasonably priced.
Haçibaba, Istiklâl Caddesi 49, Taksim, tel: (0212) 244-1886. A huge menu of specialities from all over Turkey. There is a terrace for summer dining.
Four Seasons, Istiklâl Caddesi 509, Tünel, tel: (0212) 293-3941. An English-owned restaurant with a Turkish influence. Popular for business lunches.
Pera Palas (see Where to Stay). The charming patisserie and traditional, colonial bar in this hotel were frequented by the likes of Agatha Christie and Mata Hari.

BUDGET
Çiçek Pasajı, Istiklâl Caddesi, Galatasaray. Rows of small, crowded restaurants in the 'flower passage' of the fish market, all serving meze, kebab and rakı.
Kristal Köftecisi, Istiklâl Caddesi, near the Aga Camii, tel: (0212) 245-8462. Meatballs, Arabic-style pizza and *pide* are served here.

Bosphorus
Take a taxi along the Bosphorus one night for a romantic meal in one of the many waterside restaurants. Most specialize in seafood.

Istanbul at a Glance

LUXURY

Laledan, Çırağan Palace Hotel, Çırağan Caddesi 84, tel: (0212) 258-3377. This restaurant specializes in West-coast fusion cuisine and rich desserts served in opulent luxury.

Boğaziçi, Köybasi Caddesi 10, Yeniköy, tel: (0212) 266-0071. This is a very popular Bosphorus fish restaurant which specializes in baked oysters.

MID-RANGE

Turquoise, Kurucesme Caddesi 22–24, tel: (0212) 265-8849. This restaurant is a converted boathouse in a waterside villa. It serves wonderful fish as well as international desserts.

Ali Baba, Kireçburnu Caddesi 20, Kireçburnu, tel: (0212) 262-0889. This is a wonderful place for visitors to dine on fish and meze overlooking the Bosphorus. Outdoor seating is available in summer.

Daye, Salhane Sokak 19, Ortaköy, tel: (0212) 261-8667. Home cooking is served in this handicraft gallery. There is also live Turkish music.

Sunset Grill and Bar, A. Adnan Saygun Caddesi, Kireçane Sokak, Ulus Parki 2, tel: (0212) 287-0357. Enjoy American grills and Turkish dishes in this restaurant with its stunning views over the Bosphorus.

BUDGET

A La Turka, Hazine Sokak 8, Ortaköy, tel: (0212) 258-7924. Meatballs, ravioli and stuffed pastries are specialities. Good for brunch after 10:00.

Anadolu Kavagı Village. This is a ferry lunch stop on the Asian side of the Bosphorus near the Black Sea. There are simple stalls on every pavement selling ice cream, waffles, meatballs and deep-fried mussels, as well as many basic fish restaurants.

Asian Istanbul
LUXURY

Club 29, Paşabaçe Yolu, Çubuklu, tel: (0212) 322-3888. An expensive restaurant, bar and nightclub in a stunning outdoor setting on the Bosphorus. It is open in summer only.

Denizci Restaurant, Mühürdar Caddesi 99, Kadiköy, tel: (0216) 330-1611. This classy seafood restaurant is situated in lively Kadiköy.

MID-RANGE

Café Marmara, Bağdat Caddesi 473, Suadiye, tel: (0216) 302-8752. This café serves a variety of breakfasts, snacks and pastries on its shady terrace.

Casa della Moda, Ferit Tek Sokak 15/2, Moda, tel: (0216) 418-0467. Italian specialities and pastries are served in an elegant setting.

Beylerbeyi, Beylerbeyi Iskeler Caddesi 13, Beylerbeyi, tel: (0216) 318-7004. This seafood restaurant near the Bosphorus Bridge also serves chicken and lamb.

Ethemefendi 36, Ethemefendi Caddesi 36, Kadiköy, tel: (0126) 385-4131. A pretty restaurant with a romantic garden, serving various meat and seafood dishes.

BUDGET

Ismet Baba, Icadiye Caddesi 96–98. Fresh fish and fresh fruit in wooden structure built out over the water.

Princes' Islands
There are countless small seafood restaurants and cafés around the harbours and ferry ports in the Princes' Islands.

LUXURY

Büyükada Princess, Büyükada, tel: (0216) 382-1628. Turkish specialities in the most luxurious hotel of the Princes' Islands.

MID-RANGE

Merit Halki Palas, Heybeliada, tel: (0216) 351-9550. Pretty restaurant in 19th-century hotel. Turkish specialities and great views.

Splendid Palas, Birtat Restaurant, Gullistan Caddesi 10, Buyukada, tel: (0212) 382-1245. Pretty waterside restaurant with superb fish and for dessert, great pastries.

Istanbul at a Glance

SHOPPING

Shopping is one of the greatest highlights of any visit to Istanbul, whether it is done in one of the many markets or at a modern, air-conditioned mall. The most famous market in Istanbul is the Grand Bazaar, or Kapalı Çarşı, with over 4,000 shops crammed into a labyrinth of tiny passageways, selling everything under the sun from carpets to gold, fake designer labels, brassware, onyx and leather. Another must is the nearby Spice Bazaar (Mısır Çarşısı) where you can shop for herbs, spices, condiments and other luxurious gifts such as tins of Beluga caviar.

In contrast to the hustle and bustle of the bazaars, Istanbul has several good shopping districts. Along the partly pedestrianized Istiklâl Caddesi as well as the busy Cumhuriyet Caddesi near Taksim Square are the modern designer shops, and this is also where you will find a variety of jewellery, handbag and shoe outlets. The most outstanding mall is the Akmerkez Mall, located in the suburb of Etiler. It is reputedly one of the largest shopping outlets in Europe, with a good selection of modern designer names.

Look out, too, for flea markets, food markets and open-air markets. One of the most charming is the

Sunday craft market at Ortaköy. There are a number of different flea markets in the Topkapı area; try visiting Çukurcuma Sokak in Cihangir and also Büyük Hamam Sokak in Üsküdar.

Istanbul's food markets are a real pleasure to explore. The Galatasaray Fish Market on Istiklâl Caddesi, one of the largest, is a misnomer as it sells plenty of other products besides fish. Keep a look out for caviar, crème fraiche, mushrooms, poultry (live), herbs and spices, coffee and regional cheeses as well as a huge variety of fish.

TOURS AND EXCURSIONS

Several companies operate a variety of sightseeing tours within Istanbul, although it is in fact very easy to do your sightseeing independently. At the Topkapı Palace, for example, guides are always supplied for the Harem tour, as they are for the whole of the Dolmabahçe Palace. Taking one of the many ferry boats along the Bosphorus is quite a lot cheaper than going on an organized, private boat. However, the Istanbul tour guides are very knowledgeable and there is a tremendous amount of history to discover, so a tour is a good idea if you want a more in-depth understanding of the city. You will also need to book through a private company if you want to do a

dinner cruise along the Bosphorus, which is highly recommended in summer.

Beyond Istanbul, various guided tours are organized to Bursa, Troy and Gallipoli, most of which can be done in two days, or one at a push, and also further afield, to the marvellous relics at Ephesus, to Cappadocia, and to Ankara, the capital.

Arttours, Valikonagi Caddesi 77/3, Nisantasi, tel: (0212) 231-0487, fax: (0212) 240-4945. City tours and car rental.

Plan Tours, Cumhuriyet Caddesi 131/1, 80230 Elmadag, tel: (0212) 230-8118, fax: (0212) 231-8965. City tours are offered, as well as excursions outside Istanbul, car hire, and yacht rental.

Paragon, Tesvikiye Caddesi 107/2, tel: (0212) 227-3500, fax: (0212) 227-3504. City tours and car hire.

Hot Sail Tourism & Yachting inc, Maçka, tel: (0212) 258-9983. Private Bosphorus cruises are offered, as well as tailor-made yacht cruises on the Aegean and Mediterranean seas. Motor yachts, sailing yachts and bareboat charters are available for hire.

Istanbul Vision, tel: (0212) 458-1800 for information. Istanbul's first double-decker bus tour, lasting two hours and 20 minutes, starting at Sultanahmet and visiting all the main sights.

Istanbul at a Glance

Tourist Information

Ministry of Tourism offices have several brochures and a very good map, the Istanbul City Plan, with a lot of useful information on the back. They are located all over the city:
Atatürk International Airport, tel: (0212) 573-4136;
Sultanahmet Square, tel: (0212) 518-8754;
Hilton Hotel, tel: (0212) 233-0592;
Galatasaray, Mesrutiyet Caddesi 57, tel: (0212) 243-3472.

Turkey on the Internet

Information sites include:
www.hitit.co.uk – a chatty, quirky guide to the country with lots of useful background on politics and news. www.turkey.org – the site of the Turkish Embassy in Washington, packed with information about the history and culture of the country. www.turkishdailynews.tr – a subscription-only site with on-line access to Turkey's English-language daily newspaper; very useful for business travellers.

Consulates

Canada: Büyükdere Caddesi 107/3, tel: (0212) 272-5174.
United Kingdom: Mesrutiyet Caddesi 34, tel: (0212) 293-7540.
United States: Mesrutiyet Caddesi 104/108, tel: (0212) 251-3602.

Museums

Aya Sofya, Sultanahmet, tel: (0212) 522-1750;
Military Museum, Harbiye, tel: (0212) 233-7115;
Maritime Museum, Beşiktaş, tel: (0212) 261-0130;
Sadberk Hanım Museum, Sarıyer, tel: (0212) 242-3813;
Topkapı Palace Museum, Sultanahmet, tel: (0212) 542-0480;
Yıldız Palace Museum, Beşiktaş, tel: (0212) 258-3080 ext 280;
Dolmabahçe Palace, Beşiktaş, tel: (0212) 258-5544;
Galata Tower, Sishane, tel: (0212) 245-1160.

Turkish Baths (Hamam)

A genuine hamam is cheaper and more of an experience than those in the five-star hotels. Remember to take your own towel and soap.
Cağaloğlu Hamam, Prof. Kazim Gürkan Caddesi 34, tel: (0212) 522-2424. Traditional hamam, friendly to visitors, separate sections for men and women. You can book as a group. Open 07:00–21:30 (men) and 08:00–20:00 (women).

Cemberlitas Hamam,

Vezirhan Caddesi 8, tel: (0212) 522-7974. This is an attractive, 400-year-old hamam, which is open from 06:00–24:00.

Children

Tatilya, The Republic of Fun, E-5 motorway, 18km (11 miles) west of the airport, tel: (0212) 872-5530. Tatilya is a covered entertainment centre with various rides, 12 theme areas, a lake, and children's entertainment, as well as a number of restaurants and shops.

Arts and Culture

Atatürk Cultural Center, Taksim Square, tel: (0212) 251-5600. This purpose-built opera house is shared by the opera, ballet, symphony orchestra and the State Theatre Company. It is also the venue for the Istanbul Festival in summer.
Istanbul Foundation for Culture and Arts, tel: (0212) 293-3133. This is the organizing committee for the annual film, theatre, music and jazz festivals.

ISTANBUL	J	F	M	A	M	J	J	A	S	O	N	D
AVERAGE TEMP. °F	46	47	51	60	69	77	82	82	76	68	59	51
AVERAGE TEMP. °C	8	9	11	16	21	25	28	28	24	20	15	11
HOURS OF SUN DAILY	3	5	7	6	8	7	9	10	8	6	7	4
RAINFALL in	4	4	3	2	2	1	1	1	2	3	4	5
RAINFALL mm	109	92	72	46	38	34	34	30	58	81	103	119
DAYS OF RAINFALL	18	14	14	9	8	6	4	4	7	11	14	18

Travel Tips

Tourist Information

There are branches of the **Republic of Turkey Ministry of Tourism** in the following countries: Australia, Austria, Belgium, Canada, Denmark, Finland, France, Germany, Great Britain, Israel, Italy, Japan, Kuwait, Netherlands, Russia, Singapore, Spain, Sweden, Switzerland and the USA.
Head office: Republic of Turkey Ministry of Tourism, Gazi Mustafa Kemal Bulvarı, Ankara, tel: (0312) 230-1911.
The Turkish Touring and Automobile Club, Merkez, tel: (0212) 282-8140.
Istanbul Convention and Visitors Bureau, tel: (0212) 292-1747, fax: (0212) 292-5451, e-mail: convention@superonline.com

Entry Requirements

Residents of the UK, Ireland and the USA need a **visa** to enter Turkey, which permits a stay of up to three months. Buy this at the airport on arrival; go to the **visa window** before joining the immigration queue or you will be sent back. Pay in cash (sterling or US dollars); no change is given.

Residents of Australia, New Zealand and Canada do not require a visa and may stay for up to three months. All other nationalities should check with their nearest Turkish consulate as they may require a visa in advance. Anyone entering Turkey should have at least three months still to run on their passport. Anyone wishing to stay longer than three months will need a residence **permit**; apply for one before you leave for Turkey.

Customs

Turkish ports of entry use the red and green channel system. Goods of high value should be declared as there are spot checks. **Customs allowances** are: 400 cigarettes or 50 cigars or 200g tobacco and five litres of spirits. Turkey is not yet a member of the EU, so its airport duty-free shops will continue to sell alcohol and cigarettes at duty-free prices for the forseeable future. Don't even think about smuggling **drugs** into Turkey. The penalties are harsh and life in jail is extremely tough. Likewise **antiques**; you will need

a purchase certificate to take anything resembling an antiquity, like an imitation or a piece of less than 100 years in age, out of the country. Illegal export is a serious offence.

Health Requirements

No compulsory **vaccinations** are required to enter Turkey. If you plan to travel off the beaten track in the far east of the country, tetanus, hepatitis and typhoid are recommended.

Getting There

By air: Istanbul's Atatürk Airport is the main point of entry for Turkey. Flights operate from here to all over the world and the airport is one of the two home bases of Turkish Airlines, which through its Qualiflyer alliance with other European carriers has a worldwide network. Istanbul Airlines also operates out of Istanbul, serving main European cities. A new terminal is under construction but for now, Atatürk Airport is chaotic and crowded. Claiming baggage on arrival may take up to an hour. The journey downtown takes 30–90 minutes, depending on traffic. **Buses** go every half hour from the arrivals area to Taksim Square and cost about a tenth of the price of a taxi.

By rail: Trains run from European cities, with direct services from Munich and Vienna taking around 35 hours. All trains come into Sirkeci station next to Eminönü. Trains from **Asia** and the Middle East arrive at Haydarpaşa on the Asian side.

By road: It is possible to enter Turkey by road from Bulgaria or Greece, provided the same driver takes the car out of the country within the permitted three-month stay. The main route is via the E80 motorway through Bulgaria.

By ferry: Ferries operate from Chios, Samos and Rodos in Greece to Turkish ports.

What to Pack

Istanbul can be oppressively hot in summer and damp and chilling in winter. In between, the climate is ideal. Pack for the season in which you are travelling and remember to include sturdy walking shoes for visiting the sights, as this involves a lot of standing around. Remember to include suitable clothing for holy sites. Women will need to cover heads, arms and shoulders and wear a dress of respectable length. Men will need proper shirt and trousers, not singlets and shorts. Don't forget a suitable sunblock, glasses and hat, particularly for cruising the Bosphorus. It is a good idea to pack swimwear, too. Most big hotels have a pool and you can also swim at the Princes' Islands.

Money Matters

Currency: The Turkish lira has suffered such high devaluation that you will be handed a huge wad of notes when you change money. Denominations are 5000, 10,000, 20,000, 50,000, 100,000, 250,000 and 500,000 TL. Be careful to distinguish between 50,000 and 500,000 – it is easy to confuse them.

Currency exchange: Banking hours are 08:30–12:00 and 13:30–17:00, Monday–Friday. Some bureaux de change may open on Sundays and hotels will change money any day of the week. Wait till you arrive in Turkey to change money. Not only will the rate be better but as it changes daily, usually to the traveller's advantage, there is no point in changing money weeks before. Money can be changed at banks, hotels, exchange bureaux and main post offices (PTT). You will need your passport to change cash or travellers cheques. Travellers cheques are not an ideal method of payment for goods and services as they are in, say, the USA, as some establishments are reluctant to accept them. Nor is foreign currency; although many places will accept it, the exchange rate will be appalling. Bureaux de change **(dövis bürosu)** often offer a better rate than the banks, often commission free, though not in the main tourist centres. There are many **unlicensed** change merchants in the Grand Bazaar, if you are desperate for Turkish lira, but deal with these people at your own risk. Hotel bills are settled

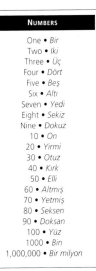

NUMBERS
One • *Bir*
Two • *İki*
Three • *Üç*
Four • *Dört*
Five • *Beş*
Six • *Altı*
Seven • *Yedi*
Eight • *Sekiz*
Nine • *Dokuz*
10 • *On*
20 • *Yirmi*
30 • *Otuz*
40 • *Kırk*
50 • *Elli*
60 • *Altmış*
70 • *Yetmiş*
80 • *Seksen*
90 • *Doksan*
100 • *Yüz*
1000 • *Bin*
1,000,000 • *Bir milyon*

in hard currency, usually US$, and if you pay by credit card, you will also be charged dollars.

Credit cards: Major credit cards are widely accepted in Istanbul, though less so in the rural areas. Diner's Club, Visa, Mastercard and American Express are most common and should work in the city's many **ATM** machines, which have English instructions on screen.

Tipping: Many restaurants will add a **service charge** of 10–15 per cent to the bill, but this is more of a cover charge and it is still customary to tip the waiter 5–10 per cent. For hotel porters, the usual rate of US$1–2 a bag is acceptable if you don't have Turkish money. **Taxi drivers** don't expect tips but it is normal to round up the amount. You should tip in a Turkish bath **(hamam)**; 20 per cent of the entrance fee to the attendant is normal.

Accommodation

Istanbul has a wide range of accommodation, from budget hostels to international five-star chains like Hilton and Hyatt. Many visitors prefer to stay in **Sultanahmet**, near the sights, as getting around the city can be time consuming. Here, most hotels are small, family-run two- and three-stars. By far the best are the 'boutique' hotels in the restored Ottoman mansions characteristic of the area. You may pay a lot for these but many of them have luxurious facilities and several have roof gardens with views of the Sea of Marmara. Business visitors tend to stay around **Taksim Square**. Here, most hotels are four- and five-star. You can save money by opting for a Turkish-run chain rather than an international group. A few of the top hotels along the **Bosphorus** have superb views but you will need to take a taxi to get downtown. There are a few **aparthotels** for visitors staying longer, and Istanbul has three approved campsites, off the main road leading out to the airport.

Eating Out

Eating out in Istanbul is a joy, with restaurants and cafés to suit all budgets and tastes. *Köftecis* and *kebapçıs* serve meatballs and kebabs, usually lamb-based, with salad, bread and a glass of *ayran*, a yoghurt drink. A *pideci* is a Turkish-style pizza restaurant. This is about as cheap as you can find. *Lokantas* or *hazır yemek* restaurants are like cafeterias – you choose ready-prepared food from a range of soups, stews and vegetable dishes. These are great value. A *restoran*, a Western-style restaurant with waiters, usually serves alcohol and is more expensive. Turkish or Ottoman *restoran* are an experience: huge assortments of *meze* as a starter, delicious grills as a main course and decadent, honey-soaked or creamy desserts. Alternatively, **street food** in and around Istanbul is delicious, be it savoury pancakes or deep-fried mussels in one of the fishing villages. If it is cooked in front of you, it should be safe to eat.

Getting Around

By Car: Car rental is expensive and you are strongly advised to use public transport within the city, as the traffic is awful and parking difficult. For trips outside the city, however, cars can be rented for weekly, daily or weekend periods. If you are proposing to drive in Turkey, you need an **International Driving Permit** and, if you are bringing your own car, third party insurance valid for both Europe and Asia.

By Boat: Boats go across the Bosphorus between the Asian and European sides. The main departure points are Eminönü, Karaköy and Beşiktaş, sailing to Üsküdar and Kadiköy on the Asian side. Ferries depart every 15 or 30 minutes, depending on the destination; the journey takes 15 minutes to Üsküdar and 25 minutes to Kadiköy. Cruises along the Bosphorus leave daily from the Eminönü jetty. The quickest way to get to the Princes' Islands is by the fast sea bus, leaving from Kabatas on the European side and taking 20 minutes to an hour, depending on which island you are visiting.

By Bus: Buses are cheap but slow. The main terminus on the European side is Taksim Square, as well as Beşiktaş and Aksaray. On the Asian side, the bus stations are at Üsküdar, Kadiköy and Bostanci. Buy a ticket at a special kiosk before you board the bus. You will have to learn to read Turkish words to use the bus as it is rare to find an English-speaking driver. A dolmuş is a shared minibus with fixed fares. Each person pays according to the distance they travel. There are dolmuş stations at Taksim Square and Aksaray and the dolmuş will wait here until they are full. It is more expensive than a bus but cheaper than a taxi and nearly as comfortable.

By Taxi: Yellow taxis are plentiful and cheap. All taxis are metered and can be hailed on the street. Watch the number of zeros carefully; while most drivers are honest, some allow a flustered passenger to hand over a note ten times larger than the meter demands. It is customary to round up the fare as a tip. Be warned that most taxi drivers chain smoke!

By Metro: Istanbul has various tram and metro lines, but none of great relevance to visitors apart from the Tünel, with just two stops from Tünel to Karaköy, the oldest tramway in Europe. Trains run every ten minutes or so and the journey is more for novelty and to avoid walking up a steep hill than a serious form of transport. A more modern metro line runs west from Aksaray, joining up with the suburban train line beyond the airport, while a second line runs east from Aksaray to Sultanahmet. A new line runs from Taksim to the suburb of Levent but is aimed mainly at commuters.

Business Hours

Turkey is a Muslim country but operates to Western working hours. Offices are open Monday–Friday, 08:00 or 09:00 to 16:00 or 17:00. Government offices may close for lunch. Shops are open Monday–Saturday 09:00–12:00 and 13:30–18:00 or 19:00; one-man shops and stalls may close briefly at prayer time. Larger mosques are always open but avoid visiting in prayer time and on Fridays, when they are busy with worshippers.

Time Difference

Istanbul is two hours ahead of GMT. Clocks move forward an hour from the end of March to the end of September, changing on a Sunday night.

Communications

Post: The main post office (PTT) is on Şehinşah Pehlevi Caddesi, west of Sirkeci railway station in Eminönü. Opening hours are 08:00–20:00 and a poste restante service is available.

Telephone: The dialling code for Turkey is 90. Istanbul's area codes are 212 for the European side and 216 for the Asian side. Buy *jeton* and *telekart* cards for making calls from payphones. These are blue and are located everywhere but if in doubt, go to Taksim Square, where there are banks of phones. Local calls are cheap, international calls expensive, particularly when marked up by hotels. Cards of all the main **calling card** companies such as AT&T, British Telecom and MCI can be used in Istanbul. Turkey has two **GSM** operators for mobile phones, Turkcell and Telsim.

Fax and e-mail: Most companies have a fax. Many have e-mail and websites. Cyber-cafés are few, but all the five-star hotels have **business centres** with Internet access and the top ones have modem points in the bedrooms, mainly on the executive floors.

Electricity

European system of 220V, 50 cycles, with two-pin plugs.

Weights and Measures

Turkey uses the metric system.

Health Precautions

There are few health hazards in Istanbul if you don't drink the water. **Diarrhoea** can strike, so take rehydrating salts with you. You may get bitten by **mosquitoes** in the Princes' Islands. Use **sunblock** when cruising on the Bosphorus and visiting tourist sites, as there can be much standing around in the sun. Minor complaints can be sorted out by a pharmacist (**eczane**) and many drugs that are prescription-only in the UK and USA are sold over the counter. Check dosages, which may be higher than at home. If taking prescription medicine, carry sufficient supplies. A **hospital** (a blue sign with a white H) offers basic free service but travellers are advised to take out medical insurance, including repatriation costs. If a woman visits a male doctor, she should take a companion, either male or female.

CONVERSION CHART		
FROM	**TO**	**MULTIPLY BY**
Millimetres	Inches	0.0394
Metres	Yards	1.0936
Metres	Feet	3.281
Kilometres	Miles	0.6214
Square kilometres	Square miles	0.386
Hectares	Acres	2.471
Litres	Pints	1.760
Kilograms	Pounds	2.205
Tonnes	Tons	0.984
To convert Celsius to Fahrenheit: x 9 ÷ 5 + 32		

Personal Safety

Istanbul is generally safe, with petty crime the main nuisance against tourists. Be vigilant in tourist areas and don't leave valuables in a hotel room. Don't wander around unfamiliar areas at night, either. **Police** officers wear blue uniforms with the word '*polis*' on them. There is a special **tourist police** force to which you report petty crime; be sure to get a written report if you need to make an insurance claim.

Women may be subject to some harassment. The rules are simple: don't dress provocatively and be polite but firm if you are followed or pestered. Rape and violent crime are rare. Be careful on Istanbul's **roads**; always assume cars have right of way, even if they don't, and be aware that Turkey has one of the highest rates in the world for motor vehicle accidents. Until 1999, the terrorist activities of the **Kurdistan Workers Party (PKK)** had not affected tourist areas for several years but with the unrest following the capture of the movement's

leader, **Abdullah Öcalan**, an urban bombing campaign resumed. Check the press before you leave (the UK Foreign Office website is a good source at www.fco.gov.uk). Be vigilant in crowded areas and report any suspect packages immediately.

Emergencies

Ambulance, tel: 112
Police, tel: 155
Fire, tel: 110
Telephone enquiries, tel: 118
Tourist police, tel: (0212) 527-4503

Etiquette

It is an offence to meddle with the Turkish **flag** or to defame the name of **Atatürk** or the **Turkish Republic**. Pointing, showing the sole of your foot, picking your teeth and kissing in public are considered rude. **Homosexuality** is illegal, but there are some gay bars, listed in the Spartacus International Gay Guide. Dress respectfully in **mosques**. Women should cover head, shoulders, upper arms and legs, while men

should not dress in shorts and singlets. Always remove shoes before entering a mosque (leave them on the shelves at the door) and don't disturb people who are praying. Avoid mosques during prayer times, on Fridays and during **Ramazan** (Ramadan). **Bargaining** in markets and bazaars (and for larger items like carpets in shops) is a way of life and not considered rude. It is also customary to accept the **apple tea** or rakı that is offered when you are making a purchase.

Language

Turkish is relatively simple, but can be hard work for a casual visitor. It is phonetically pronounced and there are some accents that you should know:

â   add a y sound to the preceding consonant
ı   pronounced 'u' as in 'full'
ö   pronounced 'ur', as in 'her'
ü   'ew' as in 'yew'
ç   'ch' as in 'church'
g   hard, as in 'go'
ğ   silent
ş   'sh' as in 'sheet'

GOOD READING

Lord Kinross (1990) *Atatürk, the Rebirth of a Nation*. Definitive biography of the father of the Turks. Weidenfeld and Nicolson.
Freely, John (1996) *Istanbul, the Imperial City*. Viking. Fascinating historical account of the city.
Sumner-Boyd, Hilary and Freely, John (1988) *Strolling Through Istanbul*. KPI Paperbacks. The classic walking guide to the famous buildings of Istanbul.
Kelly, Laurence (1987) *Istanbul – a traveller's companion*. Constable. Literary guide through the ages.
Norwich, John Julius (1995) *Byzantium, the Decline and Fall*. Readable and informative account. Viking.
Goodwin, Godfrey (1992) *A History of Ottoman Architecture*. Classic guide to Ottoman architecture. Thames and Hudson.
Seal, Jeremy (1995) *A Fez of the Heart*. Picador. Entertaining account of what it means to be a modern Turk.

INDEX

Note: Numbers in **bold**
indicate photographs